Shipowners of Cardiff

A CLASS BY THEMSELVES

1   Members of the Cardiff and Bristol Channel Incorporated Shipowners' Association pictured after their Annual General Meeting on 18 July, 1997.
From left to right; David Jones, Douglas Reid, Hubert Wilson, Philip Thomas, Stuart Reid, David Jenkins (secretary), David Ellis (Chairman), Hugh Williams, Andrew Bell (Vice-Chairman), Andrew Reid, Desmond Williams, Tony Bevan. Unable to be present was Richard Williams.
(Ronald Turner Photography, Cardiff)

Shipowners of Cardiff

A CLASS BY THEMSELVES

A History of the Cardiff and Bristol
Channel Incorporated Shipowners'
Association

DAVID JENKINS

UNIVERSITY OF WALES PRESS in association with
THE NATIONAL MUSEUMS & GALLERIES OF WALES
CARDIFF • 1997

British Library Cataloguing-in-Publication Data
A catalogue record for this book is available from the British Library.

ISBN 0–7083–1433–3

Typeset at the University of Wales Press
Printed in Great Britain by Bookcraft Ltd, Midsomer Norton

This book is dedicated to Cardiff's remaining shipowners

Cardiff is not only a coaling and shiprepairing port, but a considerable shipowning centre as well. Her shipowners constitute a class by themselves. They are fully imbued with the spirit of the old-time merchant adventurers and will not lightly brook any interference with their plans.

Cardiff, 1921 (*Syren and Shippimg*, London)

In Cardiff at dawn the sky is moist and grey
And the baronets wake from dreams of commerce,
With commercial Spanish grammar on their tongues;
And the west wind blows from the sorrowful seas,
Carrying Brazilian and French and Egyptian orders,
Echoing the accents of commercial success,
And shaking the tugs in the quay . . .

Idris Davies, *Gwalia Deserta* III
(Reproduced by kind permission of Ceinfryn and Gwyn Morris)

Contents

List of Illustrations

Preface

In my thirty-year career as a member of staff of the National Museum of Wales, I was never happier than in those years between 1978 and 1987 when I served as Curator of the Welsh Industrial and Maritime Museum.

Of course, in the 1970s and early 1980s, the museum stood amidst the derelict remains of a more prosperous golden era in Cardiff's dockland – the term 'Cardiff Bay' had not been invented then! In 1978, there was dereliction on a grand scale. Many of the outstanding office buildings built during the era of great wealth were in ruin and some were demolished, whilst street upon street of terraced housing that had accommodated families of countless racial backgrounds were torn down in the name of so-called 'progress', almost obliterating a vital community.

Even so, after this period of public vandalism in the so-called 'swinging sixties', something of the spirit and essence of a more flourishing past still persisted amongst the ruins. Shipowners who had not owned a vessel since the 1930s were still around and businessmen whose whole life had been concerned with the export of Welsh coal worldwide still made their daily journeys to Bute Road station. Elderly seamen of many racial types, retired trimmers and stevedores, tug masters and dock pilots, seamen's outfitters and café proprietors – not forgetting the 'ladies of the night' – could all still be found at the bottom end of Bute Street.

The quayside building of the Welsh Industrial and Maritime Museum, opened in 1977, was the first building to be erected in the area for over fifty years and I was proud to have been appointed its first resident curator. The social centre for the business community of the Docks was the Exchange Club in Mount Stuart Square, and the Coal Exchange had once been the powerhouse of commercial activity that made Cardiff 'the coal metropolis of the world'. I loved the comradeship of the Exchange Club, even though it was in its death throes in the early 1980s, and I was also proud of the fact that I was a member of the 'Docks Company of Pals': above all, I was proud to be called 'a Docksman'.

During my period as curator, I always felt that the Welsh Industrial and Maritime Museum should not only be concerned with the dead, forgotten past, with the history of technology and industrial archaeology, but that it should also make a contribution to contemporary life. For that reason, I was delighted to welcome the Cardiff and Bristol Channel Incorporated Shipowners' Association to establish its secretariat at the museum in 1986. I acted as secretary for three years and I was very conscious of the fact that although the Association was greatly diminished in its membership, it had a distinguished history and was for many decades a considerable influence on the development of the British mercantile fleet.

My successor as secretary, and a valued member of the Welsh Industrial and Maritime Museum's staff, undertook the difficult task of researching a history of the Association. Here are the results of his efforts in the form of an informative and inspiring book that adds another chapter to our knowledge and appreciation of a unique community that is rapidly changing beyond all recognition.

J. GERAINT JENKINS

Introduction and Acknowledgements

The Cardiff and Bristol Channel Incorporated Shipowners' Association is one of the oldest-established bodies of its kind in the United Kingdom. Founded in 1875 as the Cardiff Shipowners' Association, it grew to represent a body of men of crucial commercial influence at the height of the steam coal trade from ports in south Wales in the late nineteenth and early twentieth centuries. The decline in that coal trade, and the subsequent near-disappearance of shipowning in Cardiff and its sister ports, has left the Association a mere shadow of its former self. Nevertheless, it remains in existence and continues to function, albeit at a greatly reduced level of influence, and there is a certain irony in the fact that the Association's registered office is now at a museum.

It is some years since a past chairman of the Association, Mr Desmond Williams, suggested that a history of the Association be researched and written, a task that was delegated to the present author by Dr Geraint Jenkins, curator of the Welsh Industrial and Maritime Museum and the Association's secretary. I have since then been researching its history intermittently, somewhat hampered by the fact that the Association's archive (deposited with the Glamorgan Archive Service) is incomplete, particularly with regard to the first two decades of its existence, for which virtually no documentation exists. It has taken some time to piece together at least an outline of those early days from alternative sources, but I could not claim that the story is complete.

Much of the business discussed by the Association at its regular monthly meetings was often of a repetitive and humdrum nature, and it would be extremely tedious to set down a 'blow-by-blow' account of such proceedings. I have endeavoured therefore to concentrate in greater detail on significant episodes such as the reactions of the Association to the proposals to build new docks at Barry in the 1880s, the Seamen's Strike of 1911 and the 'schism' that split the Association in 1912–14. What often emerges from these episodes is the fact that during periods of tension, the Association was often anything but united in its approach to the problems it faced; at no time was this more so than during the divisive years leading up to the First World War that saw, among other things, the establishment of the short-lived rival Bristol Channel Shipowners' Association. Moreover, the annual reports and deliberations of the Association from the 1920s onwards are often a poignant comment on the gradual, though inexorable, decline of a once-great industry.

Many people have assisted me in writing this book. I owe a special debt to Mr Robin Craig for his perceptive and constructive criticisms. I also wish to thank the following: Mr Roy Fenton, the late Mr Frederick W. Jones, Mr John O'Donovan and Mr Desmond Williams. Any inaccuracies that remain are my responsibility. I am deeply grateful to the members of staff in the following institutions who have assisted me in my research: Bristol City Archives; Cardiff Central Reference Library (Local History Section); Chamber of Shipping, London; Companies House, Cardiff; Glamorgan Archive Service, Cardiff; House of Lords Record Office, Westminster; the National Library of Wales, Aberystwyth; the Public Record Office, Kew and Trinity House, London. Institutions and companies that provided financial support to enable the publication of the volume are listed elsewhere. I acknowledge the co-operation of Dr E. S. Owen-Jones, keeper, Welsh Industrial and Maritime Museum and Mrs Penny Fell, Head of Design and Publications, National Museum and Gallery, Cardiff. Mr Andrew Reid, the chairman of the Association from 1994 to 1997, deserves special thanks for the practical support that he readily organized, in particular the typing undertaken by Mrs Maureen Howells to whom I am also deeply grateful. My warm thanks to Susan Jenkins, Liz Powell and Ceinwen Jones of the University of Wales Press for their enthusiastic co-operation in the production of this volume. Photographs other than those from the archive of the Welsh Industrial and Maritime Museum are individually acknowledged. *Diolch yn fawr iawn i bawb.*

DAVID JENKINS
Secretary
Cardiff and Bristol Channel Incorporated Shipowners' Association.

May 1997

The generous financial support of the following organizations is acknowledged with gratitude:

The Associates of the Welsh Industrial and Maritime Museum
The Joseph Strong Frazer Trust
The Abbey Line Ltd.
Curnow Shipping Ltd.
Graig Shipping plc.
Charles M. Willie & Co. (Shipping) Ltd.

1 *Birth, Growth and Dissent, 1875–1918*

Cardiff was one of the boom towns of Victorian Britain. Between 1790 and 1914, it was transformed from a modest borough town and port at the lowest bridging point of the River Taff to become one of the foremost coal exporting ports in the world. In the 1780s a local customs official had been of the opinion that Cardiff would never develop as a coal exporting port, but on the eve of the First World War the Welsh ports of the Bristol Channel were as vital to world energy supplies as the ports of the Persian Gulf are today. The initial stimulus for the development of dock facilities at Cardiff had come not from the coal industry, however, but from the iron industry that had developed at centres like Merthyr Tydfil since the mid-eighteenth century. By 1794 the Glamorganshire Canal had been completed between Merthyr and Cardiff and in 1798 a sea lock was built at the lower end of the canal that enabled the trans-shipment of cargoes from barges to ocean-going sailing ships.

By the early nineteenth century, however, it had become clear that the basin was woefully inadequate for the growing trade and in the 1820s John, second Marquess of Bute (who has rightly been dubbed 'the creator of modern Cardiff') commissioned the eminent canal engineer, James Green, to produce plans for a new floating dock at Cardiff. Revised in the early 1830s, these plans were implemented in 1834 when work began on the 'Bute Ship Canal' or the Bute West Dock as it eventually came to be known. Completed in 1839, the dock was opened for traffic in October of that year, and it was indicative of the way in which coal was gradually supplanting iron as the foundation of the industrial economy of south Wales that twelve coal tips were provided along the eastern quay.

The Bute West Dock was soon a victim of its own success; the opening of the Taff Vale Railway in 1841 facilitated the transport of coal from the newly developed coalfields of the Cynon Valley, with the result that the new dock soon became congested. Proposals for a second dock to alleviate this congestion were drawn up in 1847, and despite the sudden death of the second Marquess in 1848, the Trustees continued with plans to build this new dock to the east of the first to cope with the growing demand for south Wales steam coal. Coal exports exceeded one million tons per annum in 1855, and a considerable boost to the trade was given in 1851 when the Admiralty announced its preference for Welsh smokeless steam coal as the optimum fuel for the Royal Navy's growing

2   Before the tramp steamer: wooden sailing vessels and paddle tugs in the Bute West Dock in the early 1870s.

fleet of steam-powered battleships. Spurred on by this notable develop-ment, and terrified by the prospect of losing trade to other ports, particularly Newport, the construction of the Bute East Dock was authorized by the Trustees and was completed in successive sections between 1855 and 1859. By 1862, coal exports exceeded two million tons per annum.

Despite these encouraging economic developments, Cardiff's early shipowners would appear to have been almost oblivious to the enormous commercial opportunities offered by the growing coal trade. In 1841 there were just sixty-five wooden sailing vessels registered at the port, with an aggregate gross tonnage of a mere 6,109 tons. There was a substantial increase during the 1850s and by 1861 the port had seventy-eight sailing vessels, aggregating almost 13,000 gross tons on its books. In addition, there were twenty-two steamers; however, with an average size of a mere 32 gross tons, these were almost certainly all paddle tugs.[1]

Three factors were to transform this state of affairs. Firstly, the years between 1860 and the early 1880s saw unprecedented progress in the technology of the merchant ship. The sailing vessel ruled supreme on deep-

3   The first Cardiff-registered cargo steamship was the *Llandaff*, built on the Tyne by Schlesinger & Davies in 1865. Seen here stranded near Land's End in April 1899, she was re-floated, but broken up later that year.

sea voyages well into the 1870s, but its days were already numbered because of notable developments in the efficiency of the marine steam engine. In 1865 Alfred Holt, founder of Liverpool's famous 'Blue Funnel' Line, had developed the first truly successful iron-hulled compound-engined steamer, *Agamemnon*, which could compete with a sailing vessel on the long ocean voyage to the Far East. By 1881 further economies had been achieved with the development of the triple-expansion marine steam engine which made even more efficient use of the steam produced, and by the mid-1880s such engines were being fitted in cargo ships whose hulls were built of steel rather than iron. The age of the tramp steamer had arrived.

Secondly, between 1850 and 1914, Britain's foreign trade doubled in both bulk and value. Coal was always available as an outward cargo for the UK's expanding fleet of tramp steamers, but the new steamers also needed homeward cargoes if they were to trade profitably. Britain's expanding industries and growing population necessitated the import of a wide range of raw materials and foodstuffs, and homeward trades in iron ore from northern Spain, pitwood from Bordeaux and Scandinavia, and grain from the Black Sea and (at a later date) the River Plate, all provided a significant impetus for the ownership of steamships, especially as turn-around time was decreased with the general improvement in port facilities.

The third factor was the arrival in Cardiff of the first generation of immigrant entrepreneurs, individuals of outstanding ability who were to transform the commercial life of Cardiff by their willingness to acquire and operate the new steam-powered vessels. They came from all over the British Isles and further afield, men such as John Cory from Padstow, the Morel brothers from Jersey and Charles Stallybrass from Newcastle upon Tyne, and they soon eclipsed Cardiff's established sailing shipowners, few of whom undertook the crucial transfer from sail to steam at the time.

All these factors combined to provide a remarkable stimulus for the development of steamship-owning at Cardiff, and with plentiful supplies of the world's best steam coal readily available, the port was poised upon the threshold of a golden era of the export of coal worldwide in the holds of locally owned steam-powered vessels. The first steamship to be owned locally was the *William Cory*, a vessel of 1,168 gross tons, jointly owned by the coal exporter William Cory and the coal owner John Nixon, but this vessel was registered at London, the port to which she habitually traded with Welsh coal. It was not until 1865 that the first Cardiff-owned and -registered steamship, aptly named *Llandaff*, was completed for H. J. Vellacott & Co., built by Schlesinger & Davies at Newcastle upon Tyne. The 411 gross ton vessel was the first of hundreds of tramp steamers built on the Tyne that would bear the legend 'Cardiff' on their sterns. During the 1870s, ownership of steamships at Cardiff outstripped that of sail; in 1871 there were eighty-two sailing vessels totalling 21,758 nett tons owned at the port, as opposed to fifty-four steamers totalling 6,604 nett tons; a decade later the Cardiff register recorded seventy-four sailing ships totalling 18,341 nett tons, whilst steamship figures had soared to 170 vessels totalling over 84,000 nett tons.[2] The coal trade was also expanding, with export figures exceeding three million tons for the first time in the mid-1870s.

It is against this background that the establishment of the Association in 1875 must be viewed. The origins of the Association lay within the Cardiff Chamber of Commerce that had been established in 1866 to promote and safeguard the town's growing commercial interests. Cardiff's early steamship owners were naturally prominent members of the Chamber, and by the mid-1870s some of them were beginning to draw attention to the fact that the Chamber was hopelessly over-burdened with work. At the monthly meeting held in May 1875, one shipowner, J. H. Wilson, pointed out that there had been insufficient time for the discussion of a number of important issues affecting shipowning interests, particularly the new Merchant Shipping Act and the proposed Lundy Refuge Harbour scheme. Wilson advocated 'the formation of sectional committees to promote the interest of different branches of our trade . . . in particular one for shipowners, shipbrokers, shippers and others.'[3]

It was agreed that consideration be given to this proposal at the June meeting of the Chamber, but at that meeting discussions were soon hopelessly bogged down in petty arguments over which trades deserved subcommittees to themselves.[4] No firm conclusions were drawn, and the August meeting of the Chamber was devoted largely to discussion of the 'Bill on Unseaworthy Ships' brought before Parliament by Samuel Plimsoll, MP. The general principle of the Bill was approved, but reservations were voiced by one shipowner, J. H. Wills, regarding the powers the Bill would grant to Board of Trade officials to detain ships and order surveys at the owners' expense. There was also strong condemnation of Plimsoll's assertion that large numbers of vessels left Cardiff overladen. It was the opinion of the Chamber that most of those vessels were Severn trows, the traditional sailing barge of the Severn estuary, trading in the upper Bristol Channel only. Wills concluded his comments with the words, 'it is people in inland towns that give Mr Plimsoll his support.'[5]

Such was the concern felt amongst local shipowners regarding certain proposals of Samuel Plimsoll's that a meeting was called at the Chamber of Commerce on 19 October 1875 to discuss the Bill and numerous other grievances which were of specific interest to the shipowning community.[6] Twenty shipowners attended and they elected Edward Hill as chairman; he went on to emphasize the desirability of establishing a shipowners' association at Cardiff, 'to watch over and defend the interests of shipping'. John Wilson then moved that a shipowners' association be formed at Cardiff; seconded by John Elliott, the motion was carried unanimously. A committee consisting of the chairman, together with J. H. Wilson, J. Guthrie, J. Watson, J. R. Christie, J. Hacquoil, J. H. Anning, A. T. Lucovich, J. Elliott and E. A. Capper, was elected to formulate a 'code of rules' whilst W. L. Hawkins, secretary to the Cardiff Chamber of Commerce, agreed to act as secretary to the new Association as well.

It is most unfortunate that the 'code of rules' drawn up by the Executive Committee has not survived, so that there is no indication whatsoever of the structure or the membership of the Association in its early years. It is also somewhat ironic that in its first chairman, the new Cardiff Shipowners' Association had elected a prominent businessman whose name was perhaps more immediately associated with Bristol rather than Cardiff. Edward Stock Hill was a partner in Charles Hill & Sons of Bristol, noted shipbuilders in that city and the founders of the well-known 'Bristol City Line' of steamships that operated a regular cargo liner service from Bristol to New York. The Hill family did have substantial business interests in Cardiff, however, as they had established Hill's Drydocks on the Bute East Dock in 1857 where, in addition to ship repairing, they had built five ships between 1862 and 1873. Edward Hill had crossed the Bristol Channel to Cardiff to manage these interests, making his home in Rookwood, Llandaff, which survives today as a hospital. He was to serve the Association as chairman for six years until 1881, the only chairman to occupy the office for so long a continuous period; thereafter, the tenure of the Association's chair was limited to one year (until extended to two years in 1964 and to three years in 1985).

It seems likely that Hill's resignation as chairman of the Association was precipitated by his election to the presidency of the Chamber of Shipping. It had been established in 1878 as the nationwide forum and lobbying body for shipowners' interests, and Hill had represented Cardiff's shipowners in the Chamber since its inception. The annual reports of the Chamber of Shipping indicate that Hill was an effective and conscientious representative of Cardiff interests in

4   **Sir Edward Stock Hill, who served as the Association's first chairman from 1875 until 1881. (By kind permission of the Chamber of Shipping.)**

the Chamber. In 1879–80 he led an effective campaign demanding that all pilotage authorities in the UK comprise shipowners' representatives, but his call for the creation of pension funds for seamen met with little support amongst his fellow Chamber members. Later in the 1880s he was vociferous in support of the Chamber's campaign for reductions in (if not indeed the total abolition of) light dues and he also supported the introduction of continuous discharge certificates for seamen.[7]

Following the death of the second Marquess of Bute in 1848, and the completion of the Bute East Dock in 1859 the trustees of the Bute Estate were frustrated in their desire to proceed with further dock expansion. Parliament was not willing to sanction the construction of new docks because of fears over the expenditure of such a large sum (£1.2 million) upon the estate of a minor. In the meantime, new dock facilities were being completed elsewhere, with the Ely Tidal Harbour being completed in 1859, and the Penarth Dock in 1865, both with the backing of the Taff Vale Railway. The Roath Basin was completed in 1874 but it was becoming clear that Cardiff's docks could cope with neither the steadily increasing coal traffic, nor the growing size of the steamships that were coming to dominate the coal export trade. Port congestion and the resulting delays to shipping at Cardiff became a serious problem; having invested heavily in new steamers, moreover, their owners could not afford protracted delays in port.

5   **Sail and steam: the iron steamer *Anne Thomas* was built by Palmers of Jarrow to the order of Evan Thomas, Radcliffe & Co. in 1882. In this portrait by Joseph Witham, she is shown slowing off Anglesey to pick up the Liverpool pilot.**

So serious was the congestion at the port of Cardiff, and indeed along the Taff Vale Railway, that in the late 1870s a number of Rhondda coal owners – chief amongst whom was David Davies 'the Ocean' – came together to consider the possibility of constructing a new dock at Barry, linked to the Rhondda by a new railway line. To this end a bill was promoted in 1882 and throughout 1883 parliamentary select committees gathered copious quantities of evidence from interested parties. The Cardiff Shipowners' Association had set up a subcommittee under the chairmanship of Thomas Roe Thompson to consider the proposals for a new dock, which in March 1883 had reported favourably on the scheme, commending the ease of access from the Bristol Channel, new dock machinery, lower dock charges and speedier turn-around for ships.[8] On 11 April 1883 Thompson was summoned to give evidence before the Commons select committee; his evidence can hardly be considered as impartial for he was one of the promoters of the Barry Dock & Railway Bill, but his statements nevertheless reflect the problems being faced by shipowners using Cardiff docks at that time.[9]

Thompson's submission to the select committee centred on the fact that he considered the Bute West and East Docks too small – 'those docks whose size now makes them out of date' were his exact words. This was particularly true of the Bute West Dock, in which any vessel exceeding sixteen feet laden draught could not load down to her marks. The largest ships could only get out of the docks during one hour either side of high water, leading to dreadful congestion in 'the drain' (the channel leading to the dock entrances) and Thompson quoted the instance of one ship owned by a member of the Association, drawing 25 feet 9 inches laden, that had been stuck in the Roath Basin for four days awaiting a spring tide before she could sail. This situation was being reflected in charter parties at the time, with shippers of coal stipulating up to three times the time actually needed to load a ship to insure themselves against delay, which in turn pushed up prices.

Thompson was also highly critical of the 'lop-sided' nature of the trade at Cardiff, accusing the dock management of making no attempt whatsoever to promote general cargo imports, which went instead to Bristol, Gloucester or Liverpool. One significant import trade vital to the coal industry, namely that of pitwood, was being hampered due to lack of discharging space on the quaysides at Cardiff, whilst similarly there was no space for laden vessels that had suffered damage to effect a temporary discharge of cargo whilst repairs were undertaken. Thompson went on to draw attention to the growing average size of steamers on order or on the stocks in British shipyards, steamers which when they entered service would be attracted to Barry rather than Cardiff. At one point he was cross-examined and asked how many steamers drawing more than twenty-five feet laden used the docks at Cardiff, to which he replied succinctly, 'not near as many as we shall have'. He concluded his evidence by stating that he wished no ill to the Bute interest, believing that the coal trade was expanding so rapidly that there would be plenty of traffic to sustain both ports, though only the smaller vessels would use Cardiff in the future unless its dock facilities were improved.

At least one member of the Association, however, chose to demur from the views presented by T. R. Thompson as the general consensus of the local shipowners. On 4 May 1883 Thomas Morel gave his evidence to the same select committee, evidence that amounted to a robust defence of the Bute party and the dock facilities at Cardiff.[10] Morel stated that his firm owned twenty-two steamers, not one of which had ever suffered any serious damage sailing in or out of the docks at Cardiff, and he further declared that he had no reason to be dissatisfied with the turn-around of his ships at the port. He also believed that there would be no need for a new dock at Barry once the new Roath Dock was completed at Cardiff. To what degree Thomas Morel was prompted to these comments by the fact that he held £8,000 of stock in the Taff Vale Railway is impossible to judge, but by the time of his death in 1903 he had also acquired a combined holding of debenture stocks and shares in the Barry Docks & Railways Co. Ltd., worth over £60,000.[11]

The Barry Dock and Railway Bill was passed by the Commons in November 1883, but was rejected by the Lords, reflecting the influence of the Bute faction in the Upper House. T. R. Thompson had appeared before the Lords Select Committee in July 1883,[12] and in his deposition of evidence had stated that the Bill had the general support of the Cardiff Shipowners' Association, comprising at that time twenty-one shipowners. Thompson was eager to expound the need for a new dock capable of handling the ever-increasing size of steamer being ordered by Cardiff owners at that time, emphasizing the economies of scale that could be achieved with larger vessels, 'we found that the small steamers that we owned in former times are going entirely out of date . . . we can carry much more tonnage in one bottom at the same expense'.[13] He further stated that the new Roath Dock at Cardiff would not alleviate the problem, since vessels would still have to negotiate 'the drain' to gain access to the Roath Basin Lock. Only by building a dock at Barry could a facility capable of handling the new larger steamers be provided, though it should be remembered that, by present-day standards, these ships were quite small; Evan Thomas, Radcliffe's new steamer *Walter Thomas*, completed in 1884 and the largest owned in Cardiff at that time, had a deadweight capacity of a little over 3,000 tons.

The Barry Dock and Railway Bill came before Parliament again in 1884 and despite fierce opposition from the Bute faction, it gained parliamentary assent on 14 August that year. With the benefit of hindsight, it is clear that the opinions of the local shipowners, united by their Association and ably expressed by T. R. Thompson, were a vital factor in the Bill's eventual success. Thompson's role in helping to bring about the creation of the port and town of Barry was recognized by the naming of Thompson Street in his honour[14] though strangely perhaps, this most able and persuasive of men was never elected to the chair of the Cardiff Shipowners' Association.

That year (1884) was also a significant one for the Cardiff Shipowners' Association, in that it saw the proper incorporation of the Association as 'a limited company that does not issue any invitation to the public to subscribe for shares, and having no share capital'. A Memorandum and Articles of Association were drawn up, presumably based upon the 'code of rules' originally drawn up in 1875. The formal objectives of the Association were recorded as being:

1. To watch over and defend the interests of shipping.
2. To take cognizance of all bills brought into Parliament affecting maritime commerce.
3. To use all means in its power for the removal of evils and redress of grievances, whether local or general.

6   The new dock at Barry nears completion in 1889. Opinion was divided
within the Association as to whether or not the construction of this facility
was justified at the time.

4. To collect information on matters of interest to shipowners and to
combine with other public bodies, or with individuals, for the furtherance
of those objects.
5. The doing of all such other lawful things, as are incidental or conducive to
the attainment of the above objects, provided the Association shall not
impose on its members any regulations which, if an object of the
Association, would be unlawful.[15]

It was declared in the Articles of Association that there should be an
upper limit of one hundred members, though it was within the powers of
the Association to increase this figure should it be thought desirable. An
eligible member was defined as 'a person who is a duly registered
managing owner of a steamer or steamers, ship or ships, or who is a
partner in a firm, . . . paying an annual subscription of not less than
£2. 2s. 0d. or such other sum as may from time to time be determined by
the Association'.[16]

It was further stipulated that there should be an annual general
meeting in January each year, together with a monthly general meeting.
Executive power was vested in a committee comprising the chairman,
vice-chairman and seven members of the Association, elected annually.
Voting powers at the general meetings were somewhat complicated; each
managing owner and his partner(s) could vote on the basis of 'one man,
one vote', but managing owners could also cast one vote for each ship

7 Charles Ellah Stallybrass, 1884.

that they owned, provided that it had been 'entered' with the Association upon the payment of a levy of 10*s*. 6*d*. per vessel. Little can those who drafted this somewhat cumbersome system of franchise have realized in 1884 what trouble it was destined to cause in later years.

The formal initial subscribers to the newly titled Cardiff Incorporated Shipowners' Association were the chairman, Charles Stallybrass, together with T. R. Thompson, Bernard Tellefsen, John Wilson, John Moore, John Fry and George Wills; all were prominent pioneers of steamship owning at Cardiff. The Association's registered office at 3 Dock Chambers, Bute Street, was shared with that of the Cardiff Chamber of Commerce, and W. L. Hawkins continued to serve both bodies in the office of secretary.

By 1890, both the Roath Dock at Cardiff and the new dock at Barry had been opened. Coal exports from Cardiff stood at nine million tons, whilst Barry saw exports in excess of one million tons within the first six months of its opening in July 1889. Cardiff's shipowners operated 183 steamships, with an aggregate gross tonnage in excess of 250,000 tons, reflecting the remarkable growth in shipowning at the booming coal port from the 1870s onwards, despite the depressed freight market of the 1880s.[17] Virtually all these vessels were tramp steamers that could, in theory, be chartered to carry any cargo between any ports, provided that the venture was both legal and safe.

In practice, however, most Cardiff tramps, like those owned in other British ports, tended to stick to a pattern of trade popularly known as 'coal out, grain home'. Having loaded coal in south Wales, ships would generally proceed to ports in the Mediterranean anywhere between Gibraltar and Alexandria, to discharge coal for naval bunkers or for railway companies in France, Italy and Egypt. The vessel would then steam in ballast to one of the numerous grain ports in the Black Sea, to load cereals from the Ukraine or the lower Danube Valley. These cereal cargoes were destined for northern European ports such as Dunkirk, Antwerp or Hamburg, from which the steamers would return in ballast to the Bristol Channel to load coal once more. By the first decade of the twentieth century a similar trade had also developed to the River Plate in South America, with south Wales steam coal being exported to fuel the Argentinian railways whilst the vessels returned to Europe laden with grain normally loaded at Rosario. Closer to home, there were also the

'intermediate' trades, particularly coal out to
Brittany and the Bay ports in the Bay of Biscay,
with pitwood providing a homeward cargo.

From the 1890s, it also becomes possible to look
in greater detail at the activities of the Cardiff
Incorporated Shipowners' Association, as the
minute books are available from 1890 onwards and
the printed annual reports from 1893 onwards.
Glancing at some of the earliest published reports
for 1893 and 1894, one is struck by the similarity
between the issues causing concern amongst shipowners a century ago and those that preoccupy
modern shipowners. In 1893, Cardiff's shipowners
were lobbying for the maintenance of the 7.5 per
cent allowance against income tax on the deprecia-
tion of vessels, whilst in 1894 a subcommittee was
established to consider 'the cheapest and most

8   Henry Radcliffe, 1890.

expeditious means of transferring ships to a foreign flag, . . . in view of
the harassing legislation in this country by which shipowners are greatly
handicapped'.[18]

Some things never change! Broadly speaking, however, the matters that
concerned the Association fell into three main categories: local, national
and foreign. In a port as busy as Cardiff was at that time, local matters were
many and varied. The proposed removal of the Custom House from the
dock in 1893 was strongly opposed and a warm welcome was given to its
location in a new building in Bute Place in October 1895.[19] Matters of
navigation in the busy Bristol Channel, with its prevailing south-westerlies,
massive tidal range and shifting sandbanks, were of obvious concern. The
harbour of refuge on the eastern side of Lundy, proposed in the 1870s, was
never built, but in 1899 Trinity House was lobbied to put a lighthouse on
the Monkstone, south-east of Cardiff's dock entrance; this was eventually
provided in 1903. The chief local navigational matter that concerned
members of the Association, however, was pilotage. In 1861 a new Bristol
Channel Pilotage Act was passed which swept away Bristol's monopoly on
pilotage and gave the ports of Cardiff, Newport and Gloucester the right to
establish their own pilotage authorities.[20] The authorities operated as
licensing bodies, granting competent individuals the right to operate as
pilots. They in turn were responsible for the acquisition and operation of
their distinctive sailing cutters; by 1900 there were about sixty such vessels
operating 'downalong', seeking incoming vessels that required pilots, all in
active competition with one another.

Whilst it is not certain when representatives of the Association first sat
on the Cardiff, and later the Barry pilotage authorities, there were nine

local shipowners on these Authorities by 1900. Over the years there were many minor disagreements relating to pilotage rates, but by the early 1900s, such was the discontent in the Bristol Channel and elsewhere in the UK over issues such as rates and compulsory pilotage that in 1909 the Board of Trade initiated a nationwide inquiry into the matter.

In evidence given to the inquiry by the Association's delegation, members recorded their opposition to compulsory pilotage, believing that pilotage licences should be granted to masters and mates manning their ships. Whilst they approved of the basic principle of levying pilotage rates according to tonnage, they also claimed that the rates were quite outdated, not having been revised extensively 'since the days of wooden sailing ships'.[21] But they reserved their sternest condemnation for the system of pilotage as it existed in the Bristol Channel at that time,

> in the Bristol Channel the system is for every pilot to own his own cutter and cruise about long distances from his base. The numbers of cutters are dangerous to shipping and the system generally is obsolete. Steam vessels for pilots in the Channel would result in greater economy, reduced charges for pilotage and greater safety. Jealousy amongst pilots seems the obstacle.[22]

The rivalry amongst pilots as to who owned the finest cutter, and how well he sailed her, was legendary, of course, and this rivalry was honed each year in the annual pilots' regatta when well-known names such as Zachariah White, Frank Trott and Lewis Alexander competed against each other in a spectacular flurry of spray and spinnakers. But it was not to last, for after long deliberation, and not without considerable individual opposition, a scheme of amalgamation was adopted by Cardiff pilots in 1913. This entailed the introduction of steam pilot cutters, the pilots working a rota system and the pilotage dues to be divided equally amongst all the pilots. Newport pilots adopted a similar system in 1914, and the pressures of war forced the Barry pilots into such a system a year later.[23] The shipowners' views had prevailed.

The efficient loading of coal at Cardiff was of obvious interest to members of the Association. They had played a major part in the compilation of the Welsh Coal Charter Party of 1896, which was the legal agreement covering the foreign export of coal cargoes from south Wales ports. W. Watkin Jones of Evan Jones & Co. was the major author of this document. Much attention was paid therefore to the construction of the Queen Alexandra Dock at Cardiff and the cargo handling facilities to be installed on the new dock, opened in June 1907. In 1905 a deputation was sent to meet Sir W. T. Lewis, the Cardiff dock manager, to discuss the coal-loading devices to be fitted on the new dock's quays. The Roath Dock of 1887 had been equipped with 'Lewis–Hunter'

9   The pilot cutter *Spray* participating in a regatta, *c.*1910. The Association's opposition to the use of these fine vessels helped lead to their total demise as working boats by 1915.

10   A 'Lewis–Hunter' coaling crane in action: the box, capable of receiving the contents of a ten-ton truck, is clearly visible, as is its conical bottom which, when opened, helped in the even distribution of coal in the hold.

coaling cranes, comprising a special box suspended from a crane, capable of receiving the contents of a ten-ton coal wagon in a special loading pit. The loaded box was then swung across and lowered into the hold of the ship, where its conical bottom was opened, helping even distribution of the cargo.

This Lewis–Hunter system was much favoured by the Association members who had been disappointed to learn that it was Sir W. T. Lewis's intention to equip the new dock with hydraulic tips that simply up-ended the wagons, shooting their contents into the ship's holds via a chute – and this despite the fact that Lewis was one of the co-inventors of the crane system. Lewis, however, told members that the cranes were more expensive to install than conventional tips, and had also proved costly in terms of maintenance; their installation at the new dock would doubtless lead to increased port dues.[24]

One of the reasons why the 'Lewis–Hunter' cranes were favoured by members of the Association was that they assisted in the trimming of coal cargo within the ship's holds. By far the most influential labour organization in Cardiff's dockland was the Cardiff Coal Trimmers' Union (CCTU); formed in 1888, the trimmers were responsible for the safe stowage of coal cargoes in ships' holds. The tiny hatches and cramped 'tween decks of wooden sailing ships had made the trimmers' services indispensable, but the advent of iron and steel steamships with their larger hatches and holds led shipowners to question the need for their work. The more equable distribution of cargo imparted by the 'Lewis–Hunter' cranes added to shipowners' misgivings, as did the development of 'turret'- and 'trunk'-deck steamers in the 1890s, with both designs claiming 'self-trimming' qualities. By 1900 it was claimed by the Association that trimmers actually stowed less than 10 per cent of an average ship's cargo of coal, whilst still charging a tariff on each ton of coal loaded.[25]

The situation was complicated by the fact that the trimmers were paid in the first instance by the *shippers* of the cargo; they then claimed from the shipowners the amount paid to the trimmers, plus a farthing a ton commission. In 1890, a Trimmers' Board had been established to conciliate between the three interest groups; each group had one representative, later increased to two. The main thrust of the Association's representation on the board was the definition of 'self-trimming' vessels, on which reduced trimming rates were to be agreed. The position of the union was strengthened, however, by the conflict of interest between the coal shippers and the shipowners; the former were concerned with the way in which the coal was handled by the trimmers so as to avoid too much breakage, whilst the interests of the Association's members lay with the safe loading and rapid dispatch of vessels.[26]

Nevertheless, the Association regarded the trimmers' union with a cautious respect, realizing what has been described as their 'strategic importance' in ensuring the safety of ships, that still depended to some degree on the proper stowage of their coal cargoes.[27] This respect was well illustrated by an incident that occurred in 1897 when a vessel belonging to an unidentified member of the Association had sailed from Cardiff with the trimmers still at work below; they were put ashore on a

11   W. J. Tatem's turret-decked steamer *Wellington*: built by Doxford of Sunderland in 1905, she and her sister *Torrington*, at 9,000 deadweight tons, were the largest single-decked cargo vessels afloat at the time.

dock pilot's boat out of Barry, for which service they were charged £1. Shortly afterwards a group of Association members met the secretary of the Cardiff Coal Trimmers' Union, Samuel Fisher, who stated the grievances of his members involved in the incident, adding that the union would in future charge an additional levy of 10*s*. per man who was forced to sail outside the dock gates. The reaction of the Association was immediate and conciliatory, and a statement was issued that 'in the future, it would not countenance the treatment of trimmers in this way'.[28]

Disagreements regarding the trimming tariff continued nevertheless, especially in regard to turret- and trunk-decked vessels. The first turret-deck steamer, the patented product of Doxford's well-known Sunderland yard, had been launched in 1891, though it was not until 1904 that a Cardiff shipowner, Edward Nicholl, acquired such a vessel, the *Whateley Hall*. Trunk-deck vessels, patented by Ropner's of Stockton-on-Tees in 1896, had first appeared on the Cardiff register in 1897 when Evan

Thomas, Radcliffe & Co. took delivery of the *Llandudno*. As further 'self-trimmers' were acquired by Cardiff shipowners (by 1906, W. J. Tatem operated two of the largest type of turret-deckers owned in the UK, the *Torrington* and the *Wellington*), negotiations continued from 1901 onwards in an attempt to agree new tariffs. Proposals presented by the Trimmers' Union in July 1906 were rejected, and in October that year the Association proposed the removal of the trimming clause from the Welsh Coal Charter Party, and that Parliamentary powers be obtained to control and employ labour in the docks .[29]

What the Association was to discover early in 1907, however, was that the Cardiff Coal Trimmers' Union had succeeded in gaining the support of the coal shippers, who went so far as to state that their interests 'were drastically opposed to those of the general body of the shipowners' with regard to trimming costs and practices.[30] On 1 January 1907, they presented the jointly agreed tariff as a *fait accompli* to the Association, whose members were grudgingly forced to accept that the trimmers' ability to 'divide and rule' had proved successful, though not before they had attempted to employ non-union trimmers on one vessel loading coal at Cardiff.[31]

In comparison with some of the other great ports in Britain, such as London or Liverpool, Cardiff handled relatively little general cargo. In 1900, whilst coal exports totalled 7.5 million tons, the amount of general cargo handled – both exports and imports – was only 338,000 tons. There were, therefore, relatively few dockers at Cardiff and they worked largely on a casual basis, as and when required. Their attempts to set up any collective organization in the 1890s were fiercely opposed by Sir W. T. Lewis, who had the backing of the Association members in his stance throughout this period of time.[32]

It was to oppose the development of trade unions at sea, as well as on the waterfront, that the Shipping Federation was established in 1890, and a Cardiff District Committee was established in 1896, initially chaired by a member of the Association, Philip Turnbull. The subsequent chairmen of the local district committee were all members of the Association, and they also acted as the Association's representatives on the national committee of the Shipping Federation in London.[33]

By far the most significant dispute between capital and labour to involve the port of Cardiff and its shipowners was the Seamen's Strike of 1911. Though nationally initiated, it had many fascinating local ramifications which will be considered here. The National Sailors' and Firemen's Union of Great Britain and Ireland (NSFU) had been formed in November 1894 following the success of the Shipping Federation in pushing its predecessor, the National Amalgamated Sailors' and Firemen's Union, into voluntary liquidation earlier that year. In the following two decades, the NSFU, led by J. Havelock Wilson, fought for wage increases,

12 William James Tatem, 1907. He was elevated to the peerage in 1918, taking the title Lord Glanely.

uniform wage rates for ships in similar trades, the establishment of a manning scale and improved provisioning. However, the union was relatively weak and somewhat lacking in organization; as such it was easily opposed by the Shipping Federation and this policy was supported in turn by members of the Cardiff Incorporated Shipowners Association via the local district committee of the Federation.[34] Certainly there was no love lost between J. Havelock Wilson and Cardiff's shipowners. In October 1906, the Association went so far as to condemn the Shipping Federation for failing to press a claim for damages against Wilson that would have resulted in his bankruptcy.[35]

Despite the relative weakness of the NSFU, it is clear that J. Havelock Wilson wished to precipitate some kind of 'showdown' with shipowners in the late 1900s. There were moves to organize seamen on an international basis, via the International Transport Workers' Federation, originally founded in 1896; by 1907 the threat of internationally organized maritime labour was being taken so seriously that the establishment of an International Shipping Federation was mooted by shipowners. On 23 February 1909, Leonard McCarthy from Newcastle upon Tyne, the chief British protagonist of such a federation, addressed members of the Association at Cardiff. Some members, especially Daniel Radcliffe and W. J. Tatem, were highly enthusiastic, but many others were lukewarm towards the notion. At the next monthly meeting of the Association, held on 16 March, it was decided not to pursue the matter any further as it would be almost impossible to secure an international conformity of action amongst shipowners in different countries.[36]

By 1910, the NSFU's campaign on behalf of seamen was centred on the following issues:

1. A minimum wage, to be standard at each port.
2. Overtime payments.
3. The establishment of a conciliation board.
4. A better manning scale for vessels.
5. The abolition of the Shipping Federation's medical test, which was seen simply as an opportunity for victimization.
6. The abolition of the engagement of seamen at Shipping Federation offices.
7. Full recognition of the NSFU.[37]

13   'Volcanic and uncalled-for speeches . . .' Edward Tupper speaking from
the balcony of the Royal Hotel, Penarth, during the seamen's strike of 1911.

These proposals were rejected outright by the Shipping Federation; the
Association's delegate to the Federation's National Committee at the time
was W. Watkin Jones, who was to be a vehement opponent of any conciliation with the NSFU during the hot summer of 1911. J. Havelock
Wilson decided in view of the Shipping Federation's rejection of his
proposed reforms, that a seamen's strike should be called at all major

ports in the UK in the summer of 1911, commencing on 14 June. In May 1911 he had sent his roving representative, 'Captain' Edward Tupper, to Cardiff to commence a campaign which would culminate in the strike. Tupper was something of an enigma, whose own accounts of his background were often contradictory. He certainly had not been awarded the VC, as he often liked to claim, and it is unlikely that he was a 'captain', military, naval or otherwise. A pragmatic improviser of policy, he was also a dramatic demagogue, whose speeches from the balcony of the NSFU's office in Bute Place were a notable aspect of the strike at Cardiff. His often violent imagery horrified the shipowners and one member of the Association, W. H. Seager, condemned his 'volcanic and uncalled-for speeches'.[38]

The strike at Cardiff began with a meeting held at Neptune Park off Newport Road on 14 June; within days, Tupper was claiming that over 700 seamen had deposited their discharge books (without which they could not sail) at the NSFU offices. The dock entrances were heavily picketed, and after those ships whose crews had joined before the official start of the strike had sailed, the docks became still. One particularly ugly aspect of the dispute was racial hatred, directed particularly at Chinese seamen who tried to break the strike – 'the yellow flotsam and jetsam of the Bristol Channel', as Tupper described them.[39]

The Association was initially somewhat slow to react to the dispute. On 29 June, however, a special meeting was called to consider a letter sent by Cuthbert Laws, manager of the Shipping Federation, in which he urged owners in all ports to lay up their ships unless they could secure crewmen who held the Federation's 'ticket'. Shipowners would be compensated out of the Federation's funds in the form of a 'laying-up indemnity' set at various scales ranging from 2*d.* per ton per day for vessels under 500 gross tons up to $\frac{3}{4}$*d.* per ton per day for vessels of 2,000 gross tons or more. Members of the Association were given a week to consider, and in a further meeting held on 7 July, the scales were predictably derided as quite inadequate. Even more striking was the statement by J. T. Duncan at the meeting, suggesting the 'desirability of recognising the Union, when properly constituted'.[40] Unfortunately there is no record of the general reaction of the meeting to this statement, but it was the first sign of the somewhat ambivalent attitude that the various members of the Association were to adopt during the dispute. This was doubtless prompted largely by the fact that freight rates were showing signs of sustained improvement after almost a decade in the doldrums, and laid-up ships obviously could not take advantage of the higher rates.

In the meantime, the strike was manifesting itself in many other UK ports; by the end of June 1911, Goole, Glasgow, Hull, Liverpool, Manchester, Newcastle and Southampton were all affected, and at many of these places the dockers had come out in sympathy with the seamen.[41] Back in Cardiff, the ambivalence of the Association's members to the strike was further displayed when around 9 July, both Henry Radcliffe and Edward Nicholl had separate meetings with Tupper to discuss one of the most crucial aspects of the dispute, seamen's wages. The chameleon-like union official was soon declaiming that he had 'found a new saviour; his friend Mr. Radcliffe . . . wanted a fair deal for seamen'.[42] The Association met on 11 July to discuss a revised offer by the Shipping Federation regarding the 'laying-up indemnity' and the new figures were given a cautious welcome. However, the meeting proceeded to look at seamen's wages, with Edward Nicholl boldly opening the discussion by declaring that he was willing to pay £5 per month to British seamen. He was supported in his statement by Daniel Radcliffe. Other owners were more cautious; Owen Williams thought £4.10s. per month to be ample. Nicholl's proposal was put to the vote and he was roundly defeated; leaving the meeting in something of a temper, he declared that they had 'lost a chance to end the strike the following morning'.[43]

Tensions heightened in Cardiff following this failed bid to resolve the dispute. On 10 July the Shipping Federation supply ship, the *Lady Jocelyn*, moored in Penarth Roads, carrying Federation-recruited crews who were ready to break the strike; there were fierce disputes within the docks over the loading and crewing of two steamers, the *Annan* and the *Foreric*, whilst on 16 July there was a running battle in the fields near Swanbridge as NSFU members successfully prevented further recruits for the *Lady Jocelyn* embarking. Tupper was arrested for intimidating a tug-owner whose vessels had been acting as tenders to the *Lady Jocelyn*; he appeared in court on the morning of 18 July. That afternoon there occurred the first serious clashes between strikers and the police as, amongst other incidents, the *Annan* was cut adrift. By 20 July, the strike was more or less general in Cardiff, with trimmers, dockers and even the employees of Spillers Mills having withdrawn their labour.[44]

Fearing an imminent Armageddon, the Lord Mayor summoned the Association's chairman, William H. Jones, and Edward Tupper (who had been released on bail) to a meeting at the City Hall. Tupper re-stated the demands of the NSFU and these demands were reported back to the Association in a special meeting held on 21 July. There was a general sentiment at the meeting that the union's demands should be granted, though it was still felt that the NSFU could not be recognized until properly constituted. The Association's representative on the Shipping Federation, W. Watkin Jones, was in a Federation meeting in London at the time, but he had made it quite clear before his departure that he was implacably opposed to any negotiation whatsoever with the NSFU until the strike was called off. During the meeting, however, news was brought of the progress

14 **W. Watkin Jones, 1897. One of the chief compilers of the Welsh Coal Charter Party, he was bitterly opposed to the manner in which the seamen's strike was eventually settled in 1911.**

of the strike at Hull, where the local shipowners were already in negotiation with the NSFU and were thought likely to concede to their demands. This news would appear to have undermined the resolve of the Association. One member, T. E. Morel, declared that he was 'not opposed to the principles of trades unions'. The meeting eventually resolved that a subcommittee of three – A. R. Chenhalls, J. T. Duncan and Daniel Radcliffe – should proceed to round-table talks with the Lord Mayor and Edward Tupper, 'to make the best settlement that they can'. The meeting took place that evening and on the following day the subcommittee reported back to a further special meeting of the Association, confirming that they had acceded to the union's demands.[45]

When W. Watkin Jones returned from London to discover that the representatives of the Association had not only been in direct discussions with Tupper, but had agreed to the NSFU's demands, he was incensed. He called a further special meeting for 27 July, at which he declared the meetings of 21 and 22 July unconstitutional because the 48 hours' notice required to call such meetings had not been given. He further demanded that the resolution empowering the subcommittee to enter into negotiations with Tupper be revoked. The Association eventually met again on 3 August. T. E. Morel moved that the agreement reached with the NSFU on 21–22 July 1911 be ratified; he was seconded by W. H. Seager and the motion was carried unanimously.[46] Significantly, W. Watkin Jones was not present. As the dispute had dragged on, the Association had distanced itself from the Shipping Federation in London, conceding instead to the weight of local pressures in Cardiff. The growing desire in the city was for a speedy settlement of a dispute that had become increasingly ugly as time went by.[47] On a purely pragmatic basis, moreover, the desire of shipowners to get their ships to sea at a time of improving freight rates cannot be underestimated. Local sentiment had prevailed in a nationally initiated dispute.

Numerous members of the Association were natives of Welsh-speaking coastal communities in north and west Wales, and were pillars of the Welsh chapel-going community in Cardiff. In 1906, the teaching of Welsh as a subject was made compulsory in Cardiff schools, and the matter was raised at a meeting of the Association. A number of members voiced their opposition to the teaching of Welsh, feeling that French or Spanish would be more useful; they doubtless had their eye on the recruitment of office employees who could deal with customers in those countries and their representatives at Cardiff. Their motion condemning the teaching of Welsh was carried, though not without opposition from some of the Association's Welsh-speaking members, in particular Henry Radcliffe, as ready to dissent as ever. Displaying remarkable powers of prophesy, he believed Cardiff to be 'the capital city of Wales' and that the national language should be taught in the local schools. In this he was warmly supported by William Jones, though both men also indicated that they appreciated the usefulness of certain foreign tongues in the world of commerce.[48]

Turning from local to national matters, it will be recalled that the Association was established initially to provide a forum for Cardiff's shipowners with regard to Samuel Plimsoll's 'Bill on Unseaworthy Ships' which led to the Merchant Shipping Act of 1876. Unfortunately, there is no surviving Association documentation to record such evidence as they gave regarding that legislation. The 1876 Act was superseded by a new Act in 1894, which repealed most earlier acts and reproduced their provisions in a coherent, consolidated form. Again, there is nothing to indicate what, if any, contribution was made by the Association regarding the 1894 Merchant Shipping Act, but only a year after it had been enacted, concerns were voiced in many quarters regarding perceived shortcomings in the Act with reference to manning scales. The Act stated clearly the standards below which a ship was considered 'unseaworthy', but was imprecise about what constituted an 'undermanned' vessel. Accordingly, a parliamentary select committee was set up late in 1894 to inquire into, and secure, the proper manning of British merchant ships.[49]

The select committee invited representatives from shipowners' associations around the UK to give evidence, and on 26 November 1894 the Cardiff Incorporated Shipowners' Association decided that it should be represented by J. R. Christie, W. R. Corfield, John Guthrie, J. H. Hallett and Philip Turnbull; in the event it was only Christie, Corfield and Hallett who gave evidence on 7 February 1895. All three witnesses were dubious of the value of introducing statutory manning scales, with J. R. Christie stating, 'I think I would like to say generally that in my opinion you must put each ship on her own merits. A compulsory manning scale would be a disastrous thing.'[50]

He went on to say that he generally left the matter of manning to his ships' masters, who knew best how to reconcile the demands of economy and safety, adding that he had never had reason to dispute any master's decision. Both Christie and Corfield also emphasized the point that if manning scales were to be introduced, they should be introduced on an international basis, otherwise foreign competitors, employing smaller crews, would undercut British shipping with serious consequences for the pre-eminence of the Red Ensign on the world's oceans. W. R. Corfield's evidence also reflected developments in the technology of steam ships at that time, particularly the abandonment of the cumbersome yards and spars designed to carry sails. Corfield stated that it was two years since he had cut down the rigging of his three steamers, noting, however, that he had not reduced the crews of these vessels accordingly. The supposed importance of experience at sea under sail was something that exercised the minds of a number of members of the select committee, but the degree to which Cardiff's shipowners had moved away from the age of sail was reflected in J. R. Christie's pithy comment, 'we might as well say that a man, before he drives a steam locomotive, ought first to have driven a stage coach'.[51]

The general desire amongst members of the Association to continue with their own 'self-regulation' of manning on board their ships was repeatedly emphasized by the three witnesses, and summing up his submission of evidence to the select committee, W. R. Corfield made the following succinct statement: 'I man my ships to keep them in good order, I man them to work them with the truest economy, and the truest economy is to give them a good crew.'[52]

However, the report of the select committee, whilst recognizing that the vast majority of British ships were well-managed and properly manned, recommended that a manning scheme should be drawn up, and detailed schedules were prepared for both sailing vessels and steamers, stipulating the number of deckhands deemed necessary, and in the case of the latter, the number of stokers and trimmers to be carried. There is no record of any subsequent reaction by Association members to the implementation of the select committee's recommendations, and neither does there appear to have been much reaction to the 1906 Merchant Shipping Act. This was the work of David Lloyd George whilst president of the Board of Trade, and its main implication was the introduction of the Board of Trade provision scale for merchant seamen (popularly known as 'Board of Trade Whack' or 'Pound and Pint') and the provision of a cook on all vessels over 1,000 gross tons. The Association was contacted by the Chamber of Shipping in July 1906 with regard to the implementation of the provision scale, but there was no marked reaction to the Chamber's suggestion that the new scale induced waste of food on board.[53]

Members of the Association continued to play an active role in the affairs of the Chamber of Shipping. Edward (by then Sir Edward) Hill continued to act as the Association's representative in the Chamber until his death in 1902, when his place was taken by Henry Radcliffe. In 1908, members of the Association voiced their strong opposition in the Chamber to the Miners' Eight-Hour Bill, believing that it would seriously reduce the productivity of coal mines throughout the UK. Henry

Radcliffe was succeeded by his younger brother Daniel in 1909, who continued to represent the Association in the Chamber until 1922.

During the first decade of the twentieth century, there were two highly disreputable aspects of shipowning at Cardiff that aroused national opprobrium and led to parliamentary legislation to remedy the situation. Despite the fact that coal exports from the port increased from 7.5 million tons in 1900 to 10.5 million tons by 1913, the years from 1903 until 1912 were marked by a prolonged depression in freight rates. During the depths of this depression in 1907 and 1908, rates were less than half those prevailing in 1900. Well-managed shipping firms owning larger and newer vessels had little cause for undue worry at such times, but owners operating smaller and older vessels soon found that their chief assets were, in fact, transformed into considerable liabilities. With the fall in freight rates there was an accompanying fall in tonnage prices, so much so that many older vessels were actually worth less than the sums for which they were insured.

This discrepancy between actual and insured values would, in retrospect, appear to have been too much of a temptation for some Cardiff shipowners. From 1905 onwards, there were a number of highly dubious losses involving locally owned vessels whose insurance value as opposed to their actual value made them more attractive propositions at the bottom of the sea rather than trading on its surface. Losses such as those of the *Aberporth* in June 1905, the *Glanhowny* and the *Powis* in May and June 1907, the *Albion* in May 1908 and the *British Standard* in May 1910 all took place in somewhat questionable circumstances, with over-insurance 'a sinister and recurring theme' in each case.[54] The circumstances in which some of these vessels were lost would have made fine scenes in a comic opera. Having loaded iron ore at Seriphos, the *Powis* sank in a dead calm in the Aegean Sea on 20 June 1907, with the crew rowing around her in the lifeboats just to be sure that she sank! The managing owners of the *Albion* and the *British Standard* were one and the same, namely Frederick Brown. The latter vessel was actually only one month old when she was lost on her maiden voyage, following the failure of the single-ship company, whose property she was, to raise sufficient capital to cover the initial cost of the vessel. Moreover, whilst valued at £46,738, the vessel was insured for over £55,000.[55]

The port of Cardiff also became notorious for a further corrupt practice that followed on directly from these instances of over-insurance. To quote the eminent maritime historian, Robin Craig,

> it became a common enterprise in certain Cardiff circles to insure marine risks in some Cardiff-owned steamships in which the insurer had no direct pecuniary interest. The insurer took out his policy in the more or less confident expectation that the ship insured would become a casualty.[56]

When the *Albion* was lost in 1908, for instance, it was discovered by underwriters that insurances totalling almost £12,000 had been taken out against her becoming a total loss by numerous individuals who had no real interest whatsoever in the vessel. The report of the court of inquiry into the loss was hard-hitting in its condemnation of such 'policy proof on interest' (PPI) insurances, describing them as 'merely speculative gambles . . . they should be prohibited by legislation'. In another court of inquiry held over the highly dubious loss of the London steamer *Oxus* in August 1908, the instance was quoted of one retired shipmaster in Cardiff who had made a hundred guineas from the total loss policy he had taken out on the vessel; he had also 'gambled' successfully on the losses of the *Glanhowny* and the *Powis* the previous summer.[57]

Following the loss of the *Albion* and the revelation of the numerous PPI policies held by people who had no direct interest in the vessel, the matter was raised by the Association's chairman, Trevor S. Jones, in a meeting held on 11 August 1908. He noted that,

> the practice had increased very greatly, especially in Cardiff. The policies were being taken up by those who had no legitimate right to do so and had no interest in the vessel whatsoever . . . aspersions had been cast on shipowners who were not in the least interested in these outside policies.[58]

It was resolved to write to the Board of Trade on this matter, condemning the practice of taking out PPI policies, and to circulate a copy of the letter to other shipowners' associations, urging them too to bring pressure to bear upon the Board of Trade. One of the most outspoken critics on this question, however, was Edward Nicholl who repeatedly attacked the practice of gambling on the loss of ships in speeches and in letters to the press in the summer and autumn of 1908. Eventually, it was reported to the Association in a meeting held on 5 November 1908 that a national conference of shipowners, underwriters and representatives of the Board of Trade was to be convened in London on 15 December, and it was the unanimous decision of the Association to send Edward Nicholl as Cardiff's delegate to this conference. Following the conference, the president of the Board of Trade, Winston Churchill, introduced his Marine Insurance (Gambling) Policies Bill in the House of Commons on 22 April 1909, 'making it a criminal offence for any person having no insurable interest in a vessel to effect, by means of a PPI policy, a speculative insurance thereon'.[59]

The Bill received the royal assent on 20 October 1909, but as David Masters commented,

> if the evidence that brought about this Act may be taken as any criterion, it looked as though the port of Cardiff was working up quite a trade as well as

an unenviable reputation for scuttling vessels. The Act definitely stopped any outsiders from profiting by these criminal actions, but unfortunately it failed to stop men from deliberately sinking ships.[60]

Most of those shipowners whose vessels were lost in dubious circumstances between 1905 and 1910 were members of the Association; yet there is not a single reference in the Association's minutes to any of these losses, nor to the inquiries that followed, despite the prominent and detailed coverage that they received in the local and national press. Neither is there any reference whatsoever to the greatest 'flagging-out' that Cardiff ever witnessed. To quote Robin Craig once more,

15   Edward Nicholl was an outspoken critic of the highly dubious practice of 'gambling' on ship losses at Cardiff in the early 1900s.

The unsavoury reputation attached to certain Cardiff speculators had its repercussions in the London marine insurance market by the first decade of the present century. Not a few underwriters demanded an additional premium to cover Cardiff-registered vessels. This induced a number of reputable Cardiff shipowners to open London offices or branches, and to register or re-register their vessels in the port of London to avoid the odium attached to some shipowners operating in the Welsh port. It helps to account for the decline in the aggregate tonnage of ships registered at Cardiff in the years immediately before the First World War.[61]

By 1912, both the Radcliffe and Nicholl fleets (aggregating 144,000 gross tons) had been transferred to London registry, and in 1913, William Reardon Smith transferred his fleet to Bideford registry, a practice which the company continued until the early 1980s. It is often popularly supposed that this was done out of a sentimental attachment to Reardon Smith's native area,[62] but sentiment rarely figures highly in shipowning, and the timing of the transfer may also reflect a desire to remove the then odious word 'Cardiff' from the sterns of his vessels. These were matters of obvious significance which had tremendous implications for ship-owning at Cardiff, but they would appear never to have been discussed formally at any meeting of the Association. It seems probable that it was felt that some topics, due to their very nature, were best left undiscussed; or if they were discussed, then any conclusions were not disclosed.

As might be expected in a shipowners' association, numerous foreign affairs engaged members' attention over the years, though there is no evidence that anything ever came of the proposed 'flagging-out' under consideration in 1894 as a means of reducing operating costs. Many such matters that concerned the Association before 1918 reflected the regular 'coal out, grain home' trades in which most of the vessels owned by member companies were employed. The Association lobbied for improvements in dock facilities at numerous ports such as Odessa and Antwerp and responded to complaints from the Turkish authorities in 1904 that steamers from Cardiff were not adhering to the agreed lanes whilst navigating the Bosporus; needless to say, the charge was hotly denied![63] Proposed increases in port dues at Rotterdam were opposed in 1908, and during the following year there was strong opposition to a new tax of one peseta per deadweight ton on ships entering Spanish ports. The Association, co-operating with other shipowners' bodies in the UK, succeeded in reducing this tax to half a peseta, but efforts to end the tax altogether came to nought.

There were numerous disputes concerning 'mat money' in the homeward trade in grain from the Black Sea. Hardly ever at this date would a cargo of cereals loaded at a Black Sea port be a homogeneous consignment from one shipper, and it was often the case that different consignments of cereals were loaded in the same hold, separated by heavy-duty matting. It normally fell to the shipowner to purchase such matting as would be required, for which he would then be reimbursed by the shipper of the cargo. On a number of occasions between 1895 and 1903, however, grain merchants and factors at Odessa tried to force a change whereby the provision and the cost of matting became the duty of the shipowner, and these suggestions were vigorously opposed by the Association.[64] When considered realistically, however, many of the foreign matters that concerned members of the Association were of concern to all British tramp owners, and were generally dealt with on a national basis through the Chamber of Shipping, rather than the local shipowners' representative bodies.

The years immediately leading up to the outbreak of the First World War constituted the high noon of the coal trade and shipping industry in south Wales. In 1912, some twenty-two million tons of coal were exported through Cardiff, Barry and Penarth; freight rates were buoyant, whilst the Cardiff Incorporated Shipowners' Association comprised 77 member companies that controlled almost 750,000 gross tons of shipping. It is highly ironic, therefore, that whilst the port of Cardiff enjoyed the peak of its commercial success, the organization that represented its commercial élite was torn apart by internal strife. So bitter was this dispute that between 1912 and 1914, a rival shipowners' association was in existence, and it seemed at times as if a reconciliation would never be achieved.

The origin of the dispute lay in the Memorandum and Articles of Association drawn up in 1884, which stipulated that voting powers at

STILL SUPPLYING STEAM!

THE WORLD: "'Tis little Wales that keeps me spinning!"

16 'Dame Wales feeds the World!' A cartoon from the Cardiff-based
Maritime Review, 2 January 1909.

general meetings were not simply on the basis of 'one man, one vote':
each managing owner also had the right to cast one vote for each ship
that he operated, provided that he paid an annual levy of 10*s*. 6*d*. per
vessel to the Association. This stipulation had been the cause of some
dissent amongst the smaller shipowners over the years, as it placed them
at an obvious disadvantage in comparison with owners who operated
fleets of twenty or more vessels as was the case with the largest fleets
owned at Cardiff at that time.

By the late 1890s, as a result of this anomaly, many of the smaller members were refusing to pay the levy to enter their ships on the books of the Association, as it brought them no advantage whatsoever in voting rights – they could always be outvoted by the larger shipowners. The larger shipowners in turn were annoyed by what they saw as a deliberate flouting of the Association's rules, and on a number of occasions during the years 1897–9, Henry Radcliffe, in particular, was highly critical of those owners who were not entering their ships and paying the stipulated levy.[65] The controversy would appear to have receded somewhat during the ensuing decade, but in November 1911 the question was raised once more, and a special committee was established on 2 November to look into and, if necessary, revise certain clauses in the Articles of Association. The committee comprised the vice-chairman, A. R. Chenhalls (partner to Ralph Morel in R. E. Morel & Co.), Trevor Jones, W. R. Corfield, W. Watkin Jones and Arthur Mawson. On 1 December 1911 they reported back to an extraordinary general meeting of the Association with the recommendation that voting rights with regard to vessels be changed to one vote for every three vessels in place of a vote for each vessel. Uproar ensued; some of the larger owners, such as William Jones, Henry Radcliffe and W. J. Tatem, were outraged, and Radcliffe proposed a motion demanding no change in the existing voting structure. Hardly had he finished speaking than W. R. Corfield proposed a further motion, namely that voting should be limited to 'one man, one vote', regardless of the number of vessels operated. The meeting was descending into chaos, and the vice-chairman adjourned proceedings, calling a further meeting to be held on 11 December.[66]

Both camps clearly did their utmost to 'whip in' all possible support for this second extraordinary general meeting. A vote was taken on Henry Radcliffe's motion of 'no change' and the larger shipowners, with their 'vessel-weighted' vote, won easily with 142 votes against the 92 votes of the 'reformers'. The situation then remained unchanged until the annual general meeting held on 21 January 1912, at which A. R. Chenhalls experienced a dismal opening to his year as chairman by reading out a list of resignations from the Association. It was the intention of those who had resigned to set up an alternative body, the Bristol Channel Shipowners' Association, with a franchise based strictly upon the notion of 'one man, one vote', regardless of the number of ships operated.[67]

The chief shipowners who had resigned were W. R. Corfield, W. Watkin Jones, Arthur Mawson, J. W. Pyman, William Reardon Smith, Percy Samuel, Lewis and Philip Turnbull, William J. Thomas and Owen and Watkin Williams. It is notable that some of these had been amongst the chief opponents of the settlement of the 1911 strike. The new Association was registered in July 1912 and its Articles of Association, drawn up in August that year, declared its membership open to managing owners of

steamships and their fellow directors or partners, on
the payment of two guineas per annum each. As
previously declared, voting in the new Association
was to be strictly upon the basis of 'one man, one
vote'. Philip Turnbull was elected chairman and the
new Association's offices were initially located in
Boston Buildings in James Street.[68]

17   **Philip Turnbull, chairman of
the breakaway Bristol Channel
Shipowners' Association, 1912–14.**

Meanwhile in the Cardiff Incorporated Shipowners' Association, the new chairman, A. R.
Chenhalls, made it clear that he desired nothing
more during his period in the chair than to heal the
rift that had occurred and to reunite the Association. His chief opponent was Henry Radcliffe, who
was implacably opposed to any reconciliation if it
meant the deletion of a vote for each ship.
Throughout 1912, all sorts of compromise arrangements were attempted. In February J. T. Duncan
suggested one vote for every two ships, but this was
turned down. By November that year an even more
complex arrangement was suggested whereby there would be one vote for
each managing owner and partner, and one vote per two vessels (tugs
excluded) with a levy of one guinea per ship entered on the associations'
books. This was tentatively agreed to, but the Bristol Channel Shipowners'
Association made it quite clear that they would not reunite with the
Cardiff Association until any voting weighting given to vessels was
deleted.[69]

A. R. Chenhalls stepped down from the chair at the AGM held in
January 1913, his ambition unfulfilled. He was succeeded by John Cory.
Another ten months went by before the new chairman was able to report
on a meeting that he had had with the Bristol Channel Shipowners'
Association. Its chairman, Philip Turnbull, once more declared that until
the principle of 'one man, one vote' was accepted as the sole basis of
franchise by the Cardiff Incorporated Shipowners' Association, there was
no hope of reconciliation. The dogged determination of the Bristol
Channel Association eventually won the day, for in the meeting at which
John Cory reported back to the Cardiff Association on 17 November
1913, W. J. Tatem eventually proposed acceptance of the reformed
franchise in order that a reconciliation of the two associations might be
achieved. He was seconded in this by Daniel Radcliffe, whereupon Henry
Radcliffe, outraged at what he perceived to be a capitulation (supported
moreover by his younger brother!) threatened to sue the Association to
reimburse the sum that had been paid as levy on all Radcliffe ships since
1882. This rash statement proved his undoing, however; the Association

approved by a large majority the formation of a delegation to negotiate the reunification of the two associations comprising Phillip Morel, Daniel Radcliffe and W. J. Tatem.

Even having agreed to the reformed franchise, the delegation from the Cardiff Association still faced difficulties from the Bristol Channel Association. It was the wish of the latter association that both bodies be wound up, and a single new association, to be known as the Cardiff and Bristol Channel Incorporated Shipowners' Association, be established. It was now the turn of the Cardiff Association to dig in their heels; they insisted that the Bristol Channel Shipowners' Association be wound up, after which Cardiff would adopt the new integrated title. It was eventually reported that agreement had been reached on 8 January 1914 and the rift was eventually healed with the formal winding-up of the Bristol Channel Shipowners' Association on 11 April 1914.[70] Whilst it may rightly be argued that the Bristol Channel Association had held out in favour of a worthy reform, there can be little doubt that the dispute had been blown up out of all proportion. Before 1914 was over, however, the newly constituted association found itself having to come to terms with an altogether more serious conflict.

In August 1914, Britain declared war upon Germany following the invasion of Belgium, and the first Cardiff-owned ship to be lost was Reardon Smith's *Cornish City* which fell victim to the German light cruiser *Karlsruhe* on 21 September. The initial reaction of the shipowning community was one of near-paralysis as owners were uncertain of the risks involved and the insurance situation, but as the government began to charter ships to take supplies to France and to ensure coal stocks at bunkering stations, there was an unprecedented advance in freight rates.[71] Whereas in 1910 it had cost eighteen shillings per ton to ship coal from south Wales to the River Plate, this rose to £3. 17s. 6d. per ton by 1916 and it had doubled again by 1918. Vessels on government charter, however, were paid what became known as 'Blue Book' rates agreed in 1915, which were somewhat lower than those obtainable on the open market. These rates caused a good deal of dissent amongst many shipowners, as vessels of particular types, especially those designed specifically as fleet colliers, were more likely to be taken up on government charter, to the financial disadvantage of their owners. Other owners were accused of fixing their vessels on charters that kept them away from the UK, making it less likely that they would be taken on government charters after arrival at a British port.

In an attempt to overcome these problems, a system of 'proportionate requisitioning' was introduced, which attempted to seek out vessels from companies whose ships had done little, or no time, on government charters. During 1915, however, the Cardiff and Bristol Channel

18 A composite photographic portrait of the members of the Cardiff and Bristol Channel Incorporated Shipowners' Association in 1916 'Stormily' at the floor of the Exchange

The Cardiff & Bristol Channel Incorporated Shipowners' Association.

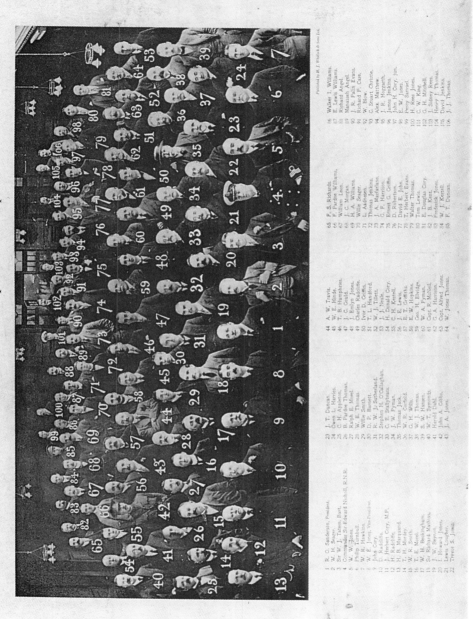

Published by R. J. Welch & Son Ltd.

1 R. O. Sanderson, President.
2 W. H. Seager.
3 Sir W. J. Tatem, Bart.
4 Commander Sir Edward Nicholl, R.N.R.
5 W. J. Jones.
6 Philip Turnbull.
7 W. R. Hawkins.
8 W. E. Jones, Vice-President.
9 John Cory.
10 D. Radcliffe.
11 Herbert Cory, M.P.
12 H. Radcliffe.
13 H. B. Marquand.
14 T. H. Morley.
15 W. R. Smith.
16 T. E. Morel.
17 H. H. Merrett.
18 Sir Richard Mathias.
19 J. W. Beynon.
20 I. Howard Jones.
21 Lewis Loughor.
22 Trevor S. Jones.

23 J. T. Duncan.
24 Owen L. Harries.
25 C. H. Appleton.
26 G. Chidgey Seaman.
27 Ralph E. Mound.
28 W. E. Thomas.
29 Willie Smith.
30 D. P. Barrett.
31 R. W. J. Sutherland.
32 Stephen H. O'Callaghan.
33 C. M. Robertson.
34 J. W. Pyman.
35 Thomas Jack.
36 W. R. Corfield.
37 G. H. Willis.
38 W. J. Thomas.
39 S. M. Hanson.
40 Sir W. Seager.
41 Harold Tuki.
42 John A. Gibbs.
43 J. A. Jones.

44 A. W. Travis.
45 W. E. Hinde.
46 T. E. B. Humphreys.
47 J. Gould.
48 J. Emrys Jones.
49 Charles Radcliffe.
50 Ivor D. Griffin.
51 T. L. Hansford.
52 W. J. Tibett.
53 J. J. Neale.
54 Donald Cory.
55 C. H. Cory.
56 J. E. Lewis.
57 E. T. Griffiths.
58 E. W. Hopkins.
59 Geo. H. Elvidge.
60 Sir A. J. Pyman.
61 S. T. Sheppard.
62 G. A. Harrison.
63 Capt. Alfred Jones.
64 W. Jones Thomas.

65 F. S. Richards.
66 F. Pardoe Williams.
67 William Leon.
68 J. C. Morgan.
69 H. A. Williams.
70 Willie Seager.
71 L. Andrason.
72 Thomas Jenkins.
73 J. A. Macfarlane.
74 G. F. Harrison.
75 Ernest G. Griffin.
76 G. H. Cory, Jun.
77 E. W. John.
78 David E. John.
79 Walter Thomas.
80 Tom Lewis.
81 E. Douglas Cory.
82 J. B. Kerr.
83 Frank Jones.
84 W. J. Kentil.
85 F. T. Duncan.

86 Walter I. Williams.
87 E. Lewis Williams.
88 Richard Angel.
89 Manansel Angel.
90 J. R. Pain Evans.
91 Richard P. Care.
92 W. Blow.
93 C. Stuart Christie.
94 Alex. Matthew.
95 J. R. Hoggarth.
96 James Jenkins.
97 J. R. Hoggarth.
98 Percy Samuel.
99 Jones.
100 C. W. King.
101 G. H. Mitchell.
102 J. Sidney Rees.
103 Harry J. Thomas.
104 David Jenkins.
105 J. J. Thomas.

19 **Key to the composite portrait of the Association's members.**

Incorporated Shipowners' Association had taken the unusual step of urging the government to impose a general limit on freight rates that would apply to all vessels, thus eliminating the differences between 'Blue Book' rates and those available on the open market.[72] The government had already taken over insurance arrangements on ships for the duration of the war, and in December 1916 the new prime minister, David Lloyd George, brought shipping under full governmental control with the creation of a Ministry of Shipping headed by the Glasgow shipowner, Sir Joseph Maclay. Lloyd George was on close terms with a number of Cardiff's more prominent shipowners (many of them later became some of his 'dreadful knights'), and it seems likely that their sentiments influenced him in his decision to establish the new ministry. The British merchant fleet was therefore 'nationalized' to all intents and purposes, with the Ministry of Shipping controlling freight rates, the construction of new standard merchant ships and the allocation of captured German tonnage for the duration of the war and for some years afterwards.

On another wartime matter, however, members of the Association took a very different view. Unease about the large profits being made by shipowners during the early months of the war led to the imposition of an Excess Profits Duty as part of the Finance Act of 1915, which provided for a levy of 50 per cent on all increases over and above pre-war profits, later increased to 80 per cent in 1917. The duty induced considerable outrage amongst members of the Association; MPs were lobbied throughout the war years, and claims were made that shipowning should be exempted on the grounds that shipowners in neutral countries were able to build up huge cash reserves that would make them formidable post-war competitors.[73] When one remembers, however, that the duty was levied on profits over and above those made during the three years prior to 1914 – which were years of vastly improved freight rates and profits – there was a degree of hypocrisy in their outcry and one only has to study the accounts of many Cardiff shipowning firms at that time to see that they had still managed to accrue considerable cash reserves. Nevertheless, in the annual report for 1917 the Association drew attention to the numerous problems that members faced in that year, 'drastic control of all tonnage, the ruthless submarine warfare, the negligible output of new standard shipping, the heavy working expenses that make it difficult for shipowners to pay their way at the existing "Blue Book" rates'.[74]

The annual report of 1917 was the first in which specific reference was made to the German 'U-boat' threat. In late 1916, and particularly in the early months of 1917, a campaign of unrestricted submarine warfare was initiated by Germany with near-disastrous results for allied shipping. A monthly average of 175,000 gross tons of shipping was sunk in the period October to December 1916, whilst in April 1917 alone, 870,000 gross

20   Sir William Seager, 1918; he later served as president of the Chamber of Shipping, 1928–9.

tons of shipping was destroyed. Whilst there are no individual loss figures for Cardiff-owned ships, many Cardiff fleets suffered heavy losses and some were totally wiped out; Evan Thomas, Radcliffe & Co., for instance, lost twenty of the twenty-eight vessels that they ran in 1914, whilst 1918 saw W. Watkin Jones's 'Field Line' without a single ship. The gallant and magnanimous conduct of many 'U-boat' commanders during the early years of the war was to some degree forgotten, particularly in the sinking of W. J. Tatem's *Torrington* on 8 April 1917. Having abandoned their torpedoed vessel, the crew were forced to leave their lifeboats and line up on the deck of U55. The master was taken prisoner below, whereupon the submarine dived, drowning all on deck.[75] The success of the 'U-boat' fleets was at last diminished, however, when Lloyd George forced a reluctant Admiralty to adopt the convoy system in mid-1917.

Another problem raised at Association meetings during the war years was the 'call-up' of skilled shipping office staff into the armed services. Although the government had taken over the direction of merchant vessels from December 1916 onwards, the individual owners were still responsible for the day-to-day running of their ships, and this became increasingly difficult as experienced staff were 'called up'. The matter was communicated to the shipping controller, though it is not known whether or not he took any action on the matter.[76] A shortage of competent office staff, and the effects of Excess Profits Duty, however, were quoted by Sir Edward Nicholl as the main reasons for the sale of his entire fleet in 1917; he had also been preoccupied with his work as chief examining officer for the Bristol Channel since 1914.[77]

The Armistice of 11 November 1918 was greeted with great optimism by the members of the Association as they looked forward to a revival in world trade and new prosperity. The end of the First World War, however, marked a turning-point in many aspects of the economic and social history of Wales, nowhere more so than in the coal and shipping industries of south Wales. The shipowners were soon to discover that their optimism was ill-founded.

2 *The Long Decline: 1918 to the Present Day*

It is an axiom that the shipping industry has always been characterized by considerable periods of prolonged depression, punctuated by short periods of intensive boom; this has, moreover, been particularly true of the tramp shipping sector. Such a boom occurred at Cardiff during the years immediately following the end of the First World War, a boom which was to have an enormous impact on the city's shipowning community. It was characterized in particular by inexperienced new-comers to the shipping industry indulging in feverish speculation, buying up individual vessels, or in some cases entire fleets, all at grossly inflated prices. But what led to this speculative frenzy, and how did it affect the Cardiff and Bristol Channel Incorporated Shipowners' Association?[1]

As has been noted, the cessation of hostilities was welcomed warmly by the Association; Germany, the great military and commercial enemy, had been defeated, and members looked forward to a relaxation of the various impositions that had been made upon the shipping industry as a result of the conflict. That which had proved the most irksome was Excess Profits Duty, which had been increased substantially in 1917. In May 1919 it was announced by the Treasury that it was to be reduced from 80 per cent to 40 per cent, and whilst the Association expressed some disappointment that it had not been totally eliminated, the Treasury's action was seen as a step towards that ultimate goal. Governmental direction of shipping and control of freight rates had also proved contentious during the latter years of the war; in March 1918, the Association had lobbied the Ministry of Shipping in an attempt to increase the 'Blue Book' rates, albeit without success.[2]

There was considerable satisfaction, therefore, amongst shipowners when it was announced in January 1919 that ships would be freed from governmental control from 1 March onwards, though it was not until October that year that the process was eventually completed. The release of ships from government control also confirmed to shipowners that proposals made by certain individuals (particularly Sir Leo Chiozza Money, parliamentary secretary to the shipping controller) to nationalize the shipping industry after the war, had come to naught.[3]

The shipyards were also freed from government regulation at this time and many shipowners were able to place orders for new buildings, using capital accumulated during the war and compensation paid out for wartime losses. During the last two years of the war, moreover, the government had embarked upon a massive construction programme to replace merchant ships lost by enemy action, with the result that in January 1919 they were able to offer for sale 137 new standard cargo steamers of varying sizes and types. The Association had already voiced concerns over the possibility of a post-war glut of tonnage when the USA had entered the war in 1917, announcing at the time that she was proposing a massive construction programme of merchant ships.[4] With the announcement of the sale of the British standard ships, members of the Association proposed that an allocation scheme be devised whereby owners who had suffered the heaviest losses be offered first option on the new buildings[5] and this idea was taken up by Lord Inchcape, who in effect acted as an agent on behalf of the government in the post-war disposal of the standard vessels.[6] Amongst the Cardiff shipping companies to take advantage of the sale was present-day Association member Graig Shipping, who purchased the 'C-type' 3,000 gross ton *War Down* in 1919.

There was a general feeling after the war – though it was not shared by all shipowners – that these new ships were needed to replace wartime losses. In actual fact the British merchant fleet in 1919 was only 700,000 gross tons less than in 1914, whilst the worldwide merchant fleet had actually grown over the same period from 42 million to over 50 million gross tons.[7] There was nevertheless an apparent shortage of available tonnage, which was actually caused by general congestion at many ports as the economy gradually reverted to a peacetime basis. One Cardiff steamer, the *Greleden*, arrived at London on 17 November 1919 but did not finish discharging her cargo until 24 January 1920,[8] whilst the Association's chairman, T. H. Mordey, made the following comments on the situation at Cardiff on 11 February 1920.

> One of the greatest troubles which the local shipowning interests have had to contend with has been the loss of earning power due to congestion. In some cases vessels with cargo have been detained two or three months before they have been able to discharge their ladings and it is . . . not an uncommon sight to see 75 or 100 vessels in the roadsteads waiting their turn to enter the docks.[9]

Problems at Cardiff were further exacerbated by the decision of the coal trimmers to work two, instead of three eight-hour shifts, a decision, according to the Association, 'propagated by a certain type of agitator'.[10] The delays thus caused to shipping meant that vessels were slow to appear on the market, leading to an apparent shortage of tonnage available for charter.

It was, therefore, a combination of many factors – post-war optimism, the halving of Excess Profits Duty, the de-regulation of shipping and an apparent shortage of available tonnage – that led to Cardiff's heady shipping boom of 1919–20. For some fifteen months, it was as if the city's shipowning community was gripped by a collective commercial madness that affected all but a hard core of older-established, sagacious owners. Even the Association was swayed by the general euphoria, noting in its annual report for 1919 the buoyant state of the shipping market and the public interest that was being generated; 'the activity of the share market is a sure sign that the public shares in our optimism'.[11] The apparent shortage of readily available tonnage pushed freight rates even higher than they had been during the war, and there was a headlong rush to establish new shipping companies to take advantage of the boom conditions. During 1919, no fewer than eighty-eight prospectuses were issued at Cardiff, mostly by new companies, but also including a few older-established enterprises seeking additional capital. The total sum sought was in excess of £7million.[12]

Tonnage prices also advanced substantially. A typical 7,500 dead-weight ton steamer which would have fetched about £42,000 in the summer of 1914 could have been sold for some £230,000 in the winter of 1919–20. It was these phenomenal prices that led some of Cardiff's most experienced shipowners to dispose of their entire fleets, demonstrating in the process their lack of faith in the long-term sustainability of the boom market. Both W. J. Tatem (recently ennobled as Lord Glanely) and W. & C. T. Jones sold their respective fleets of eight and seventeen vessels at the height of the boom, whilst W. Watkin Jones, left without ships in 1918 as a result of war losses, decided not to re-enter shipowning. Each share-holder in his company, the Field Line (Cardiff) Ltd., received £4 4s. 0d. for every £1 share held and in a final circular issued to shareholders as the company ceased trading in 1920, he described the shipping industry as being, 'burdened with so many and possibly unforeseen factors in the shape of government restrictions, financial obligations and extortionate labour demands . . . at home and abroad'.[13]

It was not just at Cardiff that certain perceptive shipowners decided to take their profit by selling their fleets on a boom market. In Newcastle upon Tyne, two of the port's foremost owners, Sir Walter Runciman and Sir Arthur Munro Sutherland, sold their respective fleets of thirteen and eleven steamers in November 1919 and February 1920. All twenty-four vessels were purchased by a Cardiff shipping company named Western Counties Shipping Ltd., promoted and managed by Edgar Edwards. Until 1915, Edwards had worked for John Cory & Sons, but he decided to enter into shipowning that year, purchasing three second-hand steamers and joining the Association at the same time. Intoxicated by the euphoria of the post-war boom, he blithely extended the capital of Western Counties, initially to £1.5 million to cover the purchase of the Runciman vessels in November 1919, then further to £2.25 million to buy the Sutherland fleet

ANOTHER SHIPPING COLLAPSE.

◆

WINDING UP OF RUMNEY STEAMSHIP CO.

VESSEL COSTING £180,000 SOLD FOR £38,000.

The directors of the Rumney Steamship Company (Limited), Cardiff, in their fourth annual report, which was issued in October last, stated that the company's bankers, who held a mortgage on the steamer Rumney, were pressing for a substantial reduction of the amount due to them. It was also intimated that the vessel was going through survey, and that when this was completed the directors would carefully consider the position of the company, and, if necessary, convene a meeting of shareholders to receive their report. Shareholders have now received the following communications:—

THE DIRECTORS' CIRCULAR.

"Your directors, in enclosing a notice of an extraordinary general meeting for the purpose of considering the liquidation of

21   Local newspapers were littered with reports such as this in the early 1920s.

in February 1920.[14] This commercial audacity surprised some, but Edwards was seen at the time as being one of the brightest morning stars in the dawn of a period of unbounded new prosperity for Cardiff shipping: 'with this go-ahead spirit, added to the value of past experience, there is no fear that Cardiff will at any time fall away from the splendid position in the shipowning sphere which it is now privileged to hold'.[15]

In the eighteen months leading up to June 1920, no fewer than 130 shipping enterprises had been promoted at Cardiff, seeking a total capital in excess of £14.5 million.[16] For a few glorious months, it looked as if the boom was anything but illusory, as shipping companies made huge profits and paid record dividends of as much as 25 per cent to delighted shareholders. Then, in the late spring of 1920, the bubble, already grossly distended, finally burst. It had gradually dawned upon the market that far from there being a shortage of tonnage, there was in fact an enormous glut, that had been added to, moreover, by the 2 million or so gross tons of shipping built since the Armistice in the UK alone. Freight rates tumbled; in February 1920 a rate of 72*s.* per ton could be obtained to ship coal from Cardiff to Genoa, but by December the 'going rate' was 19*s.* The Association's report at the end of that year belatedly recognized that 'the preponderance of available tonnage became so far in excess of requirements that from the middle of the year there was a continuous fall in freights, which are now so low that our vessels cannot be fixed, except at a loss'.[17] As freight rates fell, so did the value of tonnage; the book value of the Cardiff-owned fleet tumbled from £14.5 million in May 1920 to £8.25 million by December 1921.[18] By the summer of 1922, the price of a typical 7,500 deadweight ton steamer had fallen back to around £60,000.

The sudden onset of the slump was also compounded by adverse international economic developments. Cardiff's shipowners had always relied upon the export of Welsh coal to provide outward cargoes for their vessels, but many markets for Welsh coal had been lost during the war. Nowhere was this felt more than in the lucrative South American market, that had turned to cheaper imports from the USA after the outbreak of hostilities in Europe. Closer to home, the punitive terms of the Treaty of Versailles, which formally brought the First World War to an end, demanded that Germany make reparation to her European neighbours.

Part of this reparation was made in the form of cheap German coal supplied to France and Italy, both important pre-war customers for Welsh coal. Exports of coal to France fell from 7.25 million tons in 1913 to 5.75 million tons by 1925; exports to Italy fell from 5 million tons to 2.75 million tons during the same period.[19] The Royal Navy was moving towards oil-fired vessels, so reducing the amount of coal required for naval bunkers, whilst the homeward trade in cereals from the Black Sea's Russian ports had terminated after the Bolshevik revolution of October 1917. The situation and the general outlook can hardly have been more grim, but then in 1920 the government decided to raise the rate of Excess Profits Duty once more, from 40 per cent to 60 per cent. The Association responded with predictable outrage, declaring that, 'the excessive burden of taxation has helped reduce the shipping industry to the depths of poverty'.[20]

The combined effect of all these factors was to trigger off a prolonged slump that only receded with the outbreak of a second global conflict. The slump also brought about a merciless 'cull' of so many companies set up at the height of the boom. In a survey of the state of Cardiff's shipping industry published in 1921 by the London shipping journal, Syren and Shipping, the authors were careful to distinguish between, on the one hand, 'newer shipowning concerns which are experiencing difficulties that may perhaps prove to be of an insurmountable nature' and on the other, 'local owners . . . particularly those who have been long enough in the business to know that an industry like shipping is peculiarly susceptible to ups and downs of a more or less violent character'.[21]

The 'newer shipowning concerns' were soon tumbling like rotten apples in an autumnal gale; between 1921 and 1931, the number of shipping companies at Cardiff fell from almost 150 to 77. Those that had risen most spectacularly suffered equally dramatic collapses, none more so than Western Counties. By April 1922 a group of Edgar Edwards' creditors had issued a winding-up order upon the hopelessly over-extended enterprise. When the ships were sold, their prices averaged about a sixth of the sum that Edwards had paid for them barely two years previously – and many of them were bought back by Runciman and Sutherland, the canny Tyneside shipowners whose remarkable foresight of the movements of the shipping market netted them a substantial fortune at the time. There were other similar disasters. In February 1924, the Rumney Steamship Co. Ltd. sold its only vessel for £38,000 (having purchased her for £180,000 in 1919), whilst the Town Line went to the wall a few months later with a deficit balance in excess of £250,000. In May 1925, the massive shipping and shipbuilding conglomerate established by James Childs Gould – Goulds Steamships and Industrials Ltd. – also ceased trading, with a deficit in the region of a staggering

£750,000.[22] In 1922, the Association's chairman, Frederick Jones, remarked in the annual report,

> it is not surprising to find that a number of shipping enterprises have gone into liquidation, involving heavy losses to both creditors and shareholders . . . particularly those companies floated during and just after the war, when enormous capital outlay was involved in the purchase of vessels at unduly inflated prices.[23]

The rise and fall of so many short-lived shipping firms actually had relatively little effect at the time on the Association itself, for many of these companies were in business for so brief a period that their principals never became members. Their collapse was particularly catastrophic, however, for the hundreds of small investors who had sunk their savings in many of these companies, only to see their investments wiped out, within a few months in some instances. Indeed, few Cardiff shipping companies were to pay regular dividends over the next two decades, and those that did reflected well upon the commercial skills of their managing owners. These owners represented an earlier and more experienced generation of shipowners, who not only survived, but also profited from this unsettling cycle of boom and slump. By fixing their vessels on time charters at the top of the market, or by selling part or all of their fleets and waiting for the market to fall before ordering or purchasing replacement tonnage, they were well placed to survive the slump that followed.

That these competent and accomplished shipowners seem to have taken this difficult period in their stride is reflected in the fact that the hugely fluctuating shipping market of the early 1920s was barely discussed at any meeting of the Association. Although reference was often made in the chairman's annual address to the prevailing situation, there was never any attempt made to influence the market in any way, nor to interfere in its inexorable workings as it readjusted itself ruthlessly from late 1920 onwards. Only factors that might hinder its natural operation, such as the incidence of Excess Profits Duty, became matters for discussion, and such external influences were opposed vigorously.[24]

Whether or not it was realized at the time, however, the boom and slump of 1919–20 marked a crucial turning-point in the history of shipowning at Cardiff. The contracting market for south Wales steam coal, the increased running costs of ships and an expanded worldwide merchant fleet chasing the same volume of trade as had existed pre-war, were ominous portents for the future in the early 1920s. As the decade wore on, the annual reports of the Association's chairmen reflected increasing frustration: year after year, hoped-for signs of recovery came to naught. In 1925, for instance, the Association's annual report declared that, 'the industry is still suffering from the most serious depression ever experienced . . . the basic reason for this is too many ships and too few cargoes'.[25]

Membership of the Association was to fall away sharply during the inter-war years. Having peaked in 1921 at 149 individual members, it was to fall to eighty-four by 1931 and still further to fifty-nine by 1941. Nevertheless, the declining membership was never discussed at any meeting of the Association during these years, and the four guineas annual subscription (increased from the original two guineas in 1916) was only increased (to five guineas) in 1947.

Ironically enough, political and industrial unrest at home and abroad occasionally brought a glimmer of commercial hope to Association members in the 1920s. The French occupation of the Ruhr in 1923 had paralysed coal production in that area and led to a slight revival in trade, as did a strike by anthracite miners in the USA two years later, when much Welsh anthracite was shipped across the Atlantic, chiefly from Swansea. The General Strike of 1926 was not joined by the National Union of Seamen, and good freights were to be obtained in the import of coal from the USA to the UK at that time. The end of the strike also saw a lively demand for ships in the interrupted grain trade from the River Plate. But by 1929, the predictions were gloomy once more,

> the period under review proved most disappointing for the shipping industry . . . shipowners have had to face a continuous, but sometimes sudden, drop in freight rates in all the trades of the world . . . at the time of writing, the situation is the worst experienced for many years . . . good harvests in Europe have led to very low freight rates for grain from the River Plate, despite a good harvest in Argentina.[26]

One new development that aroused occasional debate at meetings of the Association during the 1920s was the growing adoption of motor propulsion at sea. It is generally accepted that the world's first successful ocean-going motor vessel was the *Selandia*, built by Burmeister & Wain of Copenhagen in 1912 for the well-known Danish East-Asiatic Line. In the early 1920s some British shipping companies, such as Silver Line and Walter Runciman's Moor Line, had acquired motor vessels; most Cardiff owners, however, remained sceptical about the new form of propulsion, contending that the triple-expansion steam engine was cheaper to build, easier to maintain and caused less vibration.

Their scepticism was borne out to a considerable degree by the experiences of Owen Williams, the first Cardiff shipowner to acquire motor vessels. In 1923 he took delivery of the 2,578 gross ton *Margretian*, built by Charles Hill & Sons of Bristol and powered by Beardmore–

22 **Owen Williams's remarkable 11,000 deadweight ton motor vessel** *Silurian*, **built in 1924 and seen here laid up at Hamburg a year later. Although she proved financially disastrous for her owner, she was a notable predecessor of the modern bulk carrier.**

Speedwell semi-diesel engines, she was intended for Williams's Golden Cross Line service to the Mediterranean. She was followed in 1925 by the far larger *Silurian*, a 6,903 gross ton motor vessel built by the Blythswood Shipbuilding Co. Ltd., of Glasgow; powered by Beardmore–Tosi engines, she was intended for deep-sea tramping.

Owen Williams's experiment proved to be a total disaster. The investment in both vessels was enormous, (with the *Margretian* alone costing £140,000), whilst freight rates remained low. Moreover, the *Margretian's* engines were totally unreliable and plagued by breakdowns. By June 1925, the four remaining vessels in the fleet (two steamers and two motor vessels) were laid up, and Williams, who had previously enjoyed an exceptionally successful career as a shipowner, was in debt to the tune of over £400,000. He had suffered the bad luck that is sometimes the lot of one adopting new and only partly-proven technology, but the *Silurian* of 1924, especially, was a remarkable pioneering motor ship; at 11,000 deadweight tons and with engines fitted aft she was a true bulk carrier built thirty years before her time. That was doubtless part of the problem, but one only has to compare the *Silurian* with a modern bulk carrier to see that Owen Williams's vision of the future was quite sound.[27]

Observing Owen Williams's experiences made members of the Association even more dubious of the merits of the motor ship. Many annual reports from 1924 onwards include references to the growing tonnage of motor vessels and oil– (as opposed to coal-) fired steamers, with members seemingly regarding these developments in much the same sort of way that the inhabitants of a medieval village would have viewed the advent of bubonic plague. Concern was regularly voiced at the long-term effects that the development of the motor vessel might have on the south Wales coal trade, though it was noted with satisfaction that in 1927, with tonnage prices having fallen back considerably, Cardiff owners had placed orders for a total of forty-one newbuildings, all of them coal-fired steamers.[28] But a sentimental loyalty to the locally-produced energy source was unlikely to last long in the face of the proven economy and the improved reliability of the motor vessel by the late 1920s. In 1927 the Association sent Frederick Jones

23   Frederick Jones, 1922.

as its delegate to a special conference in London organized by the Chamber of Shipping to discuss the relative merits of steam and motor propulsion,[29] but during the following two years, Sir William Reardon Smith took delivery of three motor vessels, two of which were products of Doxford's Sunderland yard and powered by the celebrated opposed-piston diesel engine developed by the firm in the 1920s. The days of the steamship were numbered.

The inter-war years were characterized by considerable strife between capital and labour, that came in the wake of the prolonged depression at that time. In marked contrast to the conflict of the summer of 1911, however, the National Sailors' and Fireman's Union (renamed the National Union of Seamen in 1926) pursued an extremely restrained policy in the 1920s, accepting wage reductions in 1921, 1923 and 1925, and refusing to participate in the General Strike of 1926. This policy led to some disagreements within the NUS, with consideration being given by some in 1925 to establish a more radical breakaway union. This move was dismissed by the Association as being inspired by 'a communistic party',[30] whilst the NUS was praised warmly by members in 1926 for its refusal to join the strike.[31] In other areas, however, some disputes still flared up. Reference has already been made to the decision of the coal trimmers to cease 'round the clock' working in 1920, a move condemned by the Association as contributing to port congestion at that time. Following pressure from a number of interests, the trimmers resumed twenty-four-hour working in June 1923, but by December that year they had once more refused to continue night working, much to members' annoyance. Moreover, despite having been successful, in 1913–15, in bringing about sweeping changes in pilotage which it was hoped would bring about considerable economies, the Association's members continued to dispute what they perceived to be exorbitant rates throughout the 1920s!

In 1921, legislation was passed authorizing the 'grouping' of the British railway companies into the so-called 'Big Four' – the LMS, the LNER, the Great Western and the Southern. Most of the major ports in south Wales were owned by railway companies and when the grouping legislation came into force on 1 January 1923, it gave the GWR a near-monopoly over all the ports between Newport and Fishguard, and overnight made a railway company the foremost owner and operator of docks in the world. This takeover *en bloc* of the south Wales valleys lines and their attendant dock systems had been opposed by Association members in June 1921, though they showed a remarkable lack of appreciation of railway geography when they advocated that the London, Midland & Scottish Railway (LMS) should take over the Rhymney Railway, the Cardiff Railway, the Taff Vale Railway and the Barry Railway. The Association's reasoning was that this would give the LMS control of Cardiff and Barry, thus promoting competition between the docks, but the impracticalities of such a division from a railway point of view were eventually explained to the Association by no less a person than Sir Eric Geddes, the tough Scotsman whom Lloyd George had made minister of transport with a specific brief to see the grouping legislation enacted.[32]

Having failed to have this competitive element built into the new dock ownership structure in south Wales, however, the Association proceeded to pay close attention to the dock dues charged by the new regime. As early as 1924 the GWR was accused of setting dues at a rate of 60 per cent above pre-war rates, and constant harrying by the Association paid off when in 1927 rates were reduced. Attention was then turned to another contentious point, namely 'double-docking fees'. If a ship discharged grain at Cardiff and then went round to Barry to load coal, the GWR levied dock dues at both ports, which the Association argued was quite unfair as the same company owned both dock facilities. Again, the Association's lobbying proved remarkably effective, for in 1928 it was agreed that there should be no 'double-docking fees' for movements to or from any two ports between Newport and Swansea.[33] In fairness to the GWR, however, the company did a great deal to promote the south Wales ports at a time of adverse economic conditions and invested heavily in all manner of new equipment and dockside facilities during this period.[34] It is also amusing to recall that one prominent member of the Association must have found himself in an awkward situation at times in the 1920s, since Lord Glanely (W. J. Tatem) sat on the board of the GWR!

24   Construction work on the Cardiff Bay Barrage during the autumn of 1995. The Shipowners' Association had proposed such a barrage in the 1920s. (By kind permission of Cardiff Bay Development Corporation.)

As this book is being written (1996), the barrage across the estuary of the rivers Taff and Ely, which is the central project of the Cardiff Bay Development Corporation, is beginning to assume a visible form. Yet the Shipowners' Association had proposed the construction of a barrage as early as 1920! Reference has already been made in this chapter to the congestion prevalent at various ports in 1919–20, and on 20 January 1920, the Association's chairman, T. H. Mordey, called for an increase in dock accommodation at Cardiff to alleviate this problem. He called upon local commercial interests and the Cardiff Corporation to come together, 'to see the day when the Taff and Ely would be the feeders of a great dock scheme'.[35]

Nothing came of that proposal, but in 1929 a similar scheme was once more under consideration, comprising a dam with two locks across the tidal channel between Penarth Head and the Queen Alexandra lock.[36] It was claimed that the construction of such a dam would impart two major advantages: firstly, the time around high water when vessels could enter and leave the port would be more than doubled; secondly, a considerable area then subjected to tidal ebb and flow would be made available for the construction of additional dock accommodation, particularly suitable for larger tonnage. A subcommittee was established to progress the scheme in conjunction with the Chamber of Commerce, but in view of the prevailing economic situation at that time it was eventually decided not to proceed with the scheme. The barrage that will be completed before the

25　Daniel Radcliffe, 1905; 1924.
He is seen here in academic
dress, having been conferred with
an honorary Doctorate of Law of
the University of Wales.

new millennium will be very different in concept and purpose from that envisaged by the Association in the 1920s – but it is amusing to note here how history can repeat itself!

Cardiff's shipowners – those that survived – went through a difficult period in the inter-war years. Their influence in the Chamber of Shipping in London declined somewhat, though Sir William Seager served as the Chamber's president in 1927–8 and Daniel Radcliffe served as vice-president in 1931–2. The old certainties of the 'coal out, grain home' trade were largely gone, and owners had to work hard to find remunerative employment for their ships. Cardiff tramps could be found loading rice at Saigon, phosphates at Nauru Island, sugar in the Fijian islands and timber at Archangel in the 1920s. Perhaps hoping for, rather than actually sensing, an upturn in the market, many Cardiff owners ordered new buildings from the mid-1920s onwards; the aggregate tonnage of shipping owned at the port actually peaked during those years. The hopes of local shipowners were soon to be dashed, however, by the Wall Street Crash of October 1929, which heralded four years of abject depression. The Association's annual report for 1930 made reference to such shattered hopes: 'recently, the passing of each year has been received with the hope that its successor will witness the raising of this cloud of depression . . . such hopes have never been more fervently expressed than at the end of 1930'.[37]

The situation did not improve. By June 1933, freight rates were at an all-time low. All that could be obtained for a cargo of coal from south Wales to the River Plate at that time was 8s. 6d. per ton, a stark contrast to the rate of 60s. per ton that could have been obtained in 1919. Only five of Evan Thomas, Radcliffe's sixteen steamers were trading that summer, whilst nine of W. J. Tatem's twelve vessels were laid up.[38] Sixty per cent of Cardiff-owned tonnage lay idle, whilst all around the UK, from the Scottish lochs to the River Fal, some two million gross tons of shipping swung idly at buoys. Some foreign countries reacted to the worsening situation by introducing subsidies for their merchant fleets, with 'national security' being generally cited as the reason for these financial provisions; such subsidies were roundly condemned by the Association, however, as, 'an artificial stimulant of great danger'.[39] Efforts were made by the British government at the World Monetary and Economic Conference of 1933 to bring about a 'more level playing field',

26   A typical Cardiff tramp steamer of the inter-war years was John Cory & Sons' *Coryton*, built in 1928 by Grays of West Hartlepool.

27   Sign of the times: shipping laid up at King Harry's Reach on the River Fal in Cornwall. (By kind permission of the Royal Polytechnic Society of Cornwall.)

but those countries that were subsidizing their merchant fleets refused to co-operate.[40]

Eventually, in November 1933, the Tramp Shipowners' Committee of the Chamber of Shipping made an application to the government for a subsidy of 10s. per ton on ships that were trading and 5s. per ton on laid-up vessels. A Cabinet committee was established in December and in May 1934 the British Shipping (Assistance) Act appeared as a White Paper. Eventually enacted in 1935, the so-called 'Scrap and Build' Act comprised two main provisions:

1. A £2 million subsidy for tramp shipowners in 1935, with the proviso that owners formulate a scheme of co-operation on establishing minimum freight rates.

2. The provision of loans to enable shipowners to buy obsolete tonnage for scrapping and then to place orders for newbuildings, at a ratio of two obsolete gross tons to each gross ton of newbuildings. All scrapping to be undertaken chiefly in the UK; all newbuildings to be ordered from British yards.

The Bill was criticized by the Opposition, who described it as the 'shipowners' dole', but not all shipowners were in favour of it either. Both Sir John Latta of Lawther, Latta & Co., and E. H. Watts of Watts, Watts & Co., disapproved of any governmental interference in the shipping industry.[41] These views were echoed to some degree in a meeting of the Association held on 15 May 1934 to discuss the White Paper. Particularly stern criticism of the proposed act was voiced by Idwal Williams; whilst noting that the proposals would have the beneficial effect of eliminating outdated excess tonnage, he felt, nevertheless, that those owners who took part in the scheme and acquired new tonnage would have an unfair and subsidized advantage over those owners already operating modern tonnage who chose not to participate.

Predictably, however, other members disagreed. J. E. Emlyn-Jones praised the scheme, declaring it to be 'immediate and practical Government action to keep the tramp shipping industry from disaster', and he was supported in his views by J. W. Duncan, T. E. Morel and Leighton Seager amongst others. When the matter was put to the vote, it was Idwal Williams's views that prevailed, and it was decided to forward the Association's reservations on the bill to the parliamentary committee, via the Chamber of Shipping. Having voiced his reservations about governmental interference in shipping in May, however, the Association, in a meeting held on 18 July 1934, went on to decry the proposed £2 million subsidy to tramp shipping as being too small![42] It seemed that whatever policy they pursued, the government could not win at this time!

Whatever the arguments, however, eleven new ships were built for four Cardiff shipowners under the scheme; all were steamers, apart from two motor vessels built for Reardon Smith Line. By taking advantage of the scheme, two Cardiff companies – the B. & S. Shipping Co. Ltd. and the E. R. Management Co. Ltd. – almost totally modernized their fleets within a two-year period.[43] Initial hostility to the notion of the subsidy seems gradually to have evaporated, also with a meeting of the Association held on 7 July 1936 voicing 'continued support' for the £2 million annual payment.[44] The annual report for 1936, moreover, expressed warm support for the Act of 1935 and its beneficial results to the tramp shipping sector:

28   John E. Emlyn-Jones, 1931.

(it) has undoubtedly saved the British tramp shipping industry from collapse . . . markedly increased the employment of British tramp ships and reduced unemployment amongst British seamen . . . it has also enabled the industry;
1) to re-organize itself
2) to reduce domestic competition
3) to establish co-operation through minimum freight schemes.[45]

The reduction of competition and the establishment of minimum freight rates were the responsibility of the various area committees established through the Chamber of Shipping. Representatives of the Association sat on the British Channel Area Tramp Shipping Subsidy Committee, and these meetings were normally chaired by the Association's chairman.

The following year saw an unexpected flourish of prosperity returning to the tramp shipping market and Association members gave an enthusiastic welcome to what was described as 'a period of prosperity greater than had been experienced for many years'.[46] It was estimated that the volume of trade had increased by some 15 per cent over that experienced in 1936, whilst widespread cereal crop failure in the USA led to a lively demand for tonnage to import supplies to make up the deficit. Such was the improvement in freight rates, however, that the payment of the subsidy was withheld, which led in turn to an appeal from the Association to maintain the subsidy, arguing that shipping was still in considerable economic difficulties.[47] This was soon to be confirmed when the freight market once more collapsed during 1938. Plentiful harvests worldwide meant that most countries were able to satisfy their cereal needs from domestic production, whilst it was also noted at the time that of the thirty-six million tons of coal exported from the UK in 1938, only four million tons were carried in ships flying the Red Ensign.[48]

The subsidy to tramp shipowners was withheld again in 1938, but the worsening economic situation and increasing international tension eventually led to further governmental intervention in 1939. On 28 March, the provisions of the British Shipping (Assistance) Bill of 1939 were announced by the Board of Trade, comprising:

1. A subsidy of £2.75 million per annum to be paid to all cargo shipowners for five years until 1944.
2. £10 million provision to make loans available to shipowners ordering new vessels on or after 29 March 1939. These loans were on similar terms to the 1935 Act, but with the deletion of the scrapping clause.
3. £2.5 million provision to make grants to shipowners ordering new vessels on or after 29 March 1939.
4. £10 million provision to support cargo liner owners facing subsidized foreign competition.
5. £2 million provision to purchase British-flag ships to create a 'Merchant Shipping Reserve'.[49]

It would appear that shipowners had put their misgivings about accepting governmental assistance on one side by this date, for within three weeks the Board of Trade was swamped with applications for loans or grants to construct 37 cargo liners and 110 tramps, aggregating over 700,000 gross tons![50] Thirteen applications came from Cardiff ship-owners, resulting in loans and grants towards the construction of six steamers and five motor vessels, aggregating some 54,000 gross tons.[51] A meeting was held by the Association to consider the Bill on 31 July 1939, at which senior officials from the Chamber of Shipping were present, though it seems likely that by then at least some of the applications mentioned above had already been made by Association members. By the time that these vessels were delivered, of course, war had broken out, although of the eleven newbuildings, only three became wartime losses.

Whilst the Association's activities during the 1930s were concerned chiefly with combating the effects of the prolonged depression in trade, other issues received attention as well during these years. One of the happier events occurred at the annual general meeting of 1931 when a presentation was made to Willoughby R. Hawkins who was retiring, having served as secretary to the Association (and to the Cardiff Chamber of Commerce) since 1893. It will be recalled that he had been preceded as secretary to the Association by his father, Willoughby Legay Hawkins, whilst his successor in 1931 was his son, Vernon W. Hawkins, who had been assistant secretary since 1927 and was to serve the Association until

1970. In all, three generations of the family gave almost a century of service to the Association, a remarkable record by any standards.[52] On a further lighter note, Association members were encouraged to participate in the British Ships Adoption Society, established in 1936, to promote geographical education and interest in the merchant marine amongst schoolchildren. A school would 'adopt' a ship, following its voyages around the world and noting its cargoes; many Cardiff companies also loaned models of adopted vessels to the relevant schools.[53]

There were, however, more serious matters to discuss, matters that, during a period of straitened economic circumstances such as the 1930s, could have a crucial bearing upon the overall viability of shipping companies. The question of dock economies and the dock dues charged by the GWR became a contentious issue once more in the early 1930s. Having invested heavily in numerous improvements in the late 1920s, the company found itself unable to recoup its expenditure against the depression in trade at the time. Certain economies were proposed; an attempt in 1930 to remove the coal shipping appliances from the Bute East Dock was opposed by the Association on the grounds that this would be detrimental to coasting shipowners whose vessels loaded both cargoes and bunkers at these tips.

29 (Above and opposite page) The chairman's badge of office, presented to the Association by Sir William Seager in 1934. Sir William's son, Elliot Seager, was chairman at the time.

Few objections were raised, however, when the GWR announced the closure of Penarth Dock in 1932. It was felt that this decision was justified in view of the dock's declining trade, and the Association further approved the decision of the GWR to continue maintenance of the dock. It was not actually closed to commercial traffic until 1936, but the onset of war led to its re-opening in 1940.[54]

On 27 June 1930, the Association met to consider a proposal by the GWR to increase dock dues, and voiced its unanimous opposition to any increases. On 2 December, however, the Association received a letter from James Milne, general manager of the GWR, informing members of the company's inability to continue operating and maintaining the ports at existing rates and insisting that the rates would have to be revised upwards. In a further meeting held on 28 January 1931, the Association reaffirmed its opposition to any increases in dock dues, raising a number

of highly involved and somewhat obscure legal points to bolster its case. So determined was the GWR to increase dock dues, however, that it eventually brought a bill before Parliament to determine its right to set dock dues at what were perceived to be realistic levels; as a result of this, the Association's chairman, J. E. Emlyn-Jones, and his immediate predecessor in the chair, R. H. Read, gave evidence before a Commons select committee early in 1931. The bill was eventually amended in the House of Commons with the insertion of a clause requiring the GWR to renew its dock dues according to the prevailing economic circumstances at five-yearly intervals from 1933 onwards. This would appear to have satisfied the Association and others who had contested the bill, which eventually passed unopposed through the House of Lords on 13 April 1931.[55]

The Association also continued to make strenuous efforts to reduce pilotage costs. In 1937, it lent its support to proposals to create a unitary pilotage authority covering the ports of Barry, Cardiff and Newport; an earlier scheme for an authority covering the entire Bristol Channel from Swansea to Newport, including Bristol too, had been deemed impractical. The Cardiff and Newport pilots indicated their willingness to merge in the smaller unitary authority, but the Barry pilots adamantly refused to co-operate in the scheme; this led to the eventual collapse of the proposals in June 1933. The Association then resorted to exerting pressure on the individual authorities, and was successful in obtaining reduced pilotage rates for ships arriving in ballast to be dry-docked or to take on bunkers. Increased shipping activity resulting from the 'mini-boom' of 1937 led the authorities to raise pilotage rates slightly, although this move was not opposed by the Association.[56]

Certain foreign matters also impinged upon the Association's deliberations during the 1930s. A proposal made by the French government in 1933 that all coal imported into France should be carried exclusively in French vessels was opposed vigorously, whilst in 1935, concern was expressed over the predominance of Russian vessels engaged in the import of timber from the USSR to the UK. This trade had provided a welcome respite from the depression to certain Cardiff shipowners, in particular Frederick Jones's 'Abbey Line', and it was Frederick Jones himself who urged that a clause, specifying that at least 20 per cent of

timber imported into the UK from the USSR
should be carried in British vessels, be inserted into
the Anglo-Russian Trade Agreement in 1936. The
Russian response was 'niet', but agitation on this
particular point continued for some years.[57] Con-
spicuous by its absence, however, is mention of that
most significant conflict of the 1930s, the Spanish
Civil War. Many Cardiff-owned ships were deeply
involved in the risky, yet highly profitable business of
running Franco's blockade to supply the Republican
cause, but apart from certain points regarding
protection of British vessels 'trading' to Spain by the
Royal Navy, the war went largely unmentioned.[58]

It is sometimes said that the Spanish Civil War
was an 'overture' to the more general conflict that
engulfed Europe in the autumn of 1939. The UK
declared war on Germany on 3 September follow-

30   **Idwal Williams, 1938.**

ing the latter's invasion of Poland, and whilst the early months of the war
have been described as 'the phoney war', this was certainly not the case
for the shipping industry. Within five days of the outbreak of war, the first
Cardiff-owned ship was lost, when W. J. Tatem's *Winkleigh* was torpedoed
on 8 September. The Association held an emergency meeting on 5
September 1939 to discuss the immediate practical problems facing
members and their ships; matters discussed included requisitioning of
vessels, insurance arrangements and the fitting of defensive guns.[59]

The Government acted more decisively than had been the case during
the First World War. All merchant ships and their insurance arrangements were brought under the control of the Ministry of Shipping,
though management and operation remained the responsibility of the
individual owners. Standard charter rates were established at more
realistic levels than those of the First World War 'Blue Book', allowing
shipowners a reasonable return without having to resort to the imposition
of an extraordinary tax on profits.[60] The convoy system was also
instituted from the outset of hostilities, though in the early years of the
war there was a chronic lack of suitable protection vessels, which rather
negated the effectiveness of the system. Then, in 1941, the Ministry of
Shipping was merged into a new Ministry of War Transport, established
to co-ordinate all forms of transport and to focus their activities towards
the war effort; the subsidiary Sea Transport Division was given specific
responsibility for merchant shipping.

Association members initially were not at all happy with the requisition
of their vessels and their direction by the Ministry of Shipping. At a
meeting held on 9 January 1940, numerous members voiced their

31   J. J. Thomas, who died in office on 4 June 1940.

dissatisfaction at the way in which their ability to operate independently was to be curtailed, and it was resolved to send a lengthy protest to the Shipping Minister:

> the Association views with serious alarm the policy of requisitioning all deep-sea tramp vessels . . . this will deprive the Nation of the practical knowledge and experience of shipowners . . . who have always responded loyally to any measures necessary in the national interest.[61]

The exigencies of total war, however, meant that their protest went unheeded, and Association members gradually adjusted to the changed circumstances imposed by the conflict. The Ministry of Shipping established a 'negotiation committee' to establish wartime chartering rates and insurance arrangements; it was also to act as a forum for shipowners' views, and Henry Bolter represented the Association on this committee. On 12 February 1940, war risk insurance arrangements were finally approved, whilst on 26 April – after prolonged haggling – the rate of 6s. per deadweight ton for steamers of 8,000 deadweight tons and over was agreed as the standard basic rate for wartime charter. Smaller vessels were paid proportionally more on a 'sliding scale', whilst all motor vessels commanded an extra shilling per deadweight ton. It was also confirmed that the Admiralty would cover the cost of fitting all defensive equipment to existing ships and to all newbuildings. There was some outcry at the time regarding the higher freight rates commanded by neutral ships, but as the conflict widened, this anomaly diminished.[62]

The Association suffered a grievous blow on 4 June 1940 with the sudden death of its chairman, J. J. Thomas, the only occasion in its history upon which a chairman has passed away in office. He was succeeded in the chair by the vice-chairman, Sir William ('Willie') Reardon Smith, eldest son of the company's founder (who had died in 1935). He became chairman at a time when the duties that the post involved were made increasingly onerous by the war. On 4 April 1941 he was appointed British Channel representative to the Ministry of Shipping, whilst on 9 May that year he was also appointed as the Association's representative on the newly constituted General Council of British Shipping (hereafter referred to as GCBS), a body established to better co-ordinate various shipping interests throughout the UK during the war.

Such was the competent manner in which Sir William dealt with his numerous responsibilities, that he was returned unopposed to the chair for three successive years, thus holding office for longer than any previous chairman, with the exception of the six-year term of Edward Hill at the Association's inception.

Moreover, his duties continued to multiply. From 1942 onwards, he chaired the Shipping Deferment Advisory Committee for the south Wales ports, a body that considered applications from those employed in the shipping industry for exemption from military service on the grounds that their work was vital to the war effort. This had been a matter of concern to the Association during the First World War and it had been raised again in a meeting held on 18 June 1940. The establishment of the committee was warmly welcomed, and it dealt with no fewer than 134 cases in 1942 alone. Sir William also chaired the monthly meetings of the Cargo Losses and Damages Committee for Cardiff from 1943 onwards, which, whilst it considered important cases relating to damage to ships, tips or cranes, also pursued lengthy and usually futile inquiries into the disappearance of a few sides of bacon or the filching of dunnage for firewood.[63]

32   **Sir William ('Willie') Reardon Smith, 1940–3.**

Following the fall of France in 1940, the German 'U-boat' packs began to establish themselves in new bases in Brittany that enabled them to operate far out into the north Atlantic, wreaking havoc amongst the all-important supply convoys. By the end of 1940, the UK and her allies had lost 1,281 merchant vessels, aggregating $4\frac{3}{4}$ million gross tons; by June 1941, this had increased to almost seven million tons. On 23 December 1940 the Association sent letters to the prime minister and the first sea lord, expressing concern at the lack of defensive cover for merchant vessels and the large number of vessels and seamen being lost as a result. At the time the conflict at sea was hopelessly unequal; armed trawlers and the little 'Flower' class corvettes were no match for the 'U-boats'. Though a number of south Wales ships acquitted themselves honourably with the ancient twelve-pounders mounted on their poops, deep-laden tramps designed for economy, not speed, were sitting ducks in that dreaded area in mid-Atlantic where they were beyond the range of escorts stationed in Canada or the UK. Many times in the early 1940s, the country stared into the abyss of starvation and defeat, and Churchill was later to recall that the so-called 'Battle of the Atlantic' was the one theatre of the war that caused him perpetual anxiety.[64]

The situation was alleviated considerably by the entry of the USA into the war in December 1941 following the bombing of Pearl Harbour, a development that was given a warm greeting by the Association. Perhaps the most decisive American contribution to the seaborne war effort was the construction of the 2,710 'Liberty' ships, some of which were soon to come under the management of Association members. By the early autumn of 1942, such was the scale of the Allied shipbuilding effort – the American 'Liberties', the Canadian 'Forts' and 'Parks' and the British 'Empires' – that for the first time in the war, they were able to outpace the toll of the 'U-boats'. The Allies' campaign was also helped by the development of improved detection tactics and weapons. The German submarine campaign was by no means immediately neutralized, however; the winter of 1942–3 witnessed a final 'all-out' attempt by the 'U-boat' packs to cripple the UK's supply lines, with nearly 700,000 gross tons of Allied shipping lost in March 1943 alone, thus making it one of the worst months of the conflict. In the face of these appalling wartime odds, the seamen of the Merchant Navy continued to 'occupy their business in great waters', with much the same equanimity as they faced their old and ever-present adversary, the sea itself. The Association's annual reports for the war years pay tribute to the 'sterling work' of the merchant seamen.

By May 1943, so effective had the Allies' anti-submarine measures become that Admiral Donitz decided to call off his great North Atlantic offensive. It was the crucial turning-point in the war at sea; the 'U-boats' never regained the initiative. Meanwhile preparations were being made for the invasion of Europe the following spring and there was a sense in which the beginning of the end of the war was approaching at last. In a meeting of the Association held on 27 March 1944, members were also looking forward to the end of the war and the problems that would face the shipping industry in peacetime. There was a general sentiment at this meeting that governmental aid would be necessary to finance a post-war reconstruction programme, though it seems strangely inconsistent that members were advocating such a scheme when only twenty-five years previously the large-scale construction of standard cargo ships by the government had contributed substantially towards the slump of the early 1920s. In this context, however, fears were also voiced as to the future disposal of the large numbers of standard cargo vessels – particularly the American 'Liberty' ships – that had been built during the conflict. Their potential to undermine the post-war market was enormous, and strict control of any future sale was advocated. Members also voiced their opposition towards any form of operational subsidy for peacetime trading.[65] These sentiments were forwarded to the Chamber of Shipping in London, presided over at the time by Sir Leighton Seager.

No fewer than twenty-three vessels that were either owned or managed by Association members sailed in the great fleet that set out for the Normandy beaches early in June 1944 whilst another locally owned vessel, the *Vera Radcliffe*, suffered the ignominious fate of being sunk deliberately as part of the 'Gooseberry harbour' off Juno Beach.[66] Within a year, the war in Europe was over, and the Association's report for 1945 expressed heartfelt relief at the end of the conflict. The losses, however, had been enormous. Nearly 30,000 merchant seamen had lost their lives, and of the British tramp tonnage owned in 1939, only 25 per cent remained afloat; nearly 70 per cent of Cardiff-owned tonnage had been lost. Moreover, remembering the events of the post-war period of 1919–20, it was with some caution that Association members looked forward to the newly won peace.

The caution of Association members was compounded by Labour's landslide victory at the general election of July 1945. Labour's manifesto had pledged the nationalization of numerous key industries, and the eventual decision not to nationalize shipping companies was greeted with relief. Nevertheless, the Association voiced strong opposition to the nationalization of the industries such as coal, railways, and the docks in the late 1940s, calling in 1946 for a 'National Public Enquiry' into the various proposals.[67] One aspect of government policy that did please Association members, however, was the progressive 'de-control' of shipping; by 1946, complete control had been replaced by a licensing system, whereby some ships were requisitioned and certain inward freights directed and controlled.

Much was done to alleviate fears over a post-war glut of tonnage by the decision of the US Maritime Commission to 'mothball' the vast majority of the 'Liberty' ships. Not all of them were laid up, however; in all, 127 were sold to British owners to replace war losses, though only one, the *Samdonard*, came under Cardiff ownership as Claymore Shipping's *Daybeam*. A number of Association members bought standard British-built 'Empire' ships and Canadian-built 'Fort' vessels that they had been managing previously for the Ministry of War Transport, thus at least partially making good war losses. Some dissatisfaction was voiced in 1946 that the bids of some Association members for standard tonnage had been curtailed or even rejected outright; in 1947, the aggregate gross tonnage of the Cardiff-owned fleet was 255,038, but ten years previously it had been double that figure, clearly demonstrating the critical impact of the war.[68]

Caution remained the watchword amongst local shipowners in the late 1940s, however; still haunted by the spectre of the post-First World War

33   Richard G. M. Street, 1947.

boom and slump, there was a marked reluctance to invest in newbuildings. The notable exception to this trend was Richard Street of the South American Saint Line, who in 1948 took delivery of two strikingly handsome motor vessels, the *St Essylt* and the *St Thomas*, for the company's cargo liner service to the River Plate. With the benefit of hindsight, it can be perceived that shipowners, especially those in the tramping sector, pursued what was perhaps an unnecessarily cautious policy in the post-war years. This caution was reflected in the initial willingness of Association members to participate in the Chamber of Shipping's Deep Sea Tramp Co-operative Committee, the establishment of which was first mooted in October 1946. Its main aim was to secure minimum freight rates (and lay-up rates should the situation arise), though Association members voiced opposition to some aspects of the committee's proposals, such as centralized 'fixing' of cargoes. In the event, however, the much-feared pattern of boom and slump failed to manifest itself for a number of reasons. The demand for shipping was kept buoyant by the US 'Marshall Plan', designed to assist in the restoration of war-ravaged European economies, and also by the outbreak of subsequent conflicts in the Far East, such as the Korean War of 1950–3.[69]

Shipowners at Cardiff, in common with those elsewhere in the UK, enjoyed a highly remunerative post-war decade, but the same could not be said for the port of Cardiff itself, which emerged into an uncertain post-war world whose energy requirements were met increasingly by oil rather than coal. Exports of coal from Cardiff in the late 1940s averaged only some one million tons per annum (equal only to the exports of the 1850s), whilst the nationalization of the coal industry in 1947 under-mined the local market on the Coal Exchange. During the late 1940s, Association members repeatedly expressed their concern over the 'neglig-ible' foreign demand for Welsh steam coal and the increasing tendency to 'fix' vessels on the Baltic Exchange in London. Coal exports improved slightly in 1948 following the desperate fuel shortages of the previous year, but the trend towards fixing cargoes on the London market was irreversible. Moreover, as if reflecting the growing importance of oil, the first two tankers to be owned at Cardiff were bought by Radcliffe's in 1947, the first of a number of such vessels to be operated by the company in subsequent years.[70]

Moreover, the Association itself was facing financial problems. In 1946, the individual membership fee was raised to five guineas in an attempt to

34   The striking motor cargo liner *St Essylt*, built by Thompsons of Sunderland in 1948 for the South American Saint Line.

offset a recurring annual shortfall in subscription revenue against expenditure. The Association had first incurred an operating loss of £109 18s. 9d. in 1942, followed by a small loss of almost £42 in 1943. Accordingly, it had been decided on 2 March 1944, to improve liquidity by taking £250 from the Association's £1,700 investment in $3\frac{1}{2}$% War Stock, dating from 1915. This measure provided a financial 'crutch' until the increase in subscriptions was approved in 1946. The Association's financial viability remained tenuous, however, in the face of rising costs and a largely static membership, and it was clearly impractical to continue subsidizing operational costs out of long-term capital investments.

Change was eventually precipitated in 1953, when in a meeting held on 24 August, it was reported that the Chamber of Commerce had made a request for increased financial contributions from those bodies for which it provided secretarial services. These comprised the Shipowners' Association, the Shipbrokers' Association, the Coal Exporters' Association, the Coal and Shipping Exchange, the Shipping and Forwarding Agents' Association and the Pitwood Importers' Association, which together paid £1,075 per annum to the Chamber of Commerce. The reply of the Shipowners' Association stated that they already paid £200 per annum to the Chamber of Commerce, but could not, in the prevailing circumstances, contemplate any increase in payments. The

35   **Alan J. Reardon Smith, 1954.**

Association's chairman, Alfred Jenkins, suggested, however, that members might consider the establishment of a modest tonnage levy upon ships using the ports of Cardiff and Barry, quoting a number of British and foreign ports at which similar systems were already operational. It was agreed to establish a sub-committee to investigate the matter further.[71]

The subcommittee reported back to a meeting held on 23 November 1953, recommending the establishment of a voluntary levy payable by ships docking at Cardiff and Barry, up to a maximum of three visits per annum. The system was to become operational on 1 January 1954, with the following scale of charges:

Vessels in gross tonnage	*Charge per visit*
Up to 100	1*s.* 6*d.*
101–150	2*s.* 6*d.*
151–500	5*s.*
501–1500	10*s.*
1501–3000	15*s.*
3001–4000	20*s.*
4001 and upwards	25*s.*

Disagreements ensued, however, as to the method whereby this levy should be collected; Association members were of the opinion that it should be collected by the shipbrokers on behalf of the Chamber of Commerce, whilst the Chamber believed that the whole matter should be administered by the Shipowners' Association, especially as it was initially the Association's idea. A compromise was reached eventually when it was decided to form a shipping levy committee, comprising two representatives each from the shipowners and the shipbrokers, to be chaired by the chairman of the Shipowners' Association. The proceeds of the levy were to be paid into a separate levy account, with distributions to be made at the Levy Committee's discretion. Following this delay, the levy was eventually instituted on 1 February 1954, but by mid-August it was reported that it had raised only £3 14*s.* 0*d.* This was because a considerable number of shipowners had refused to pay, among them prominent companies such as Chapmans, Ellermans, Everards, Hogarths, Shell, Stag Line and Stephenson Clarke. The Admiralty had also objected to paying the levy on Royal Naval vessels on courtesy visits. Local agents and brokers had refused, moreover, to approach their principals on the matter, declaring it to be the duty of the Association to contact those owners opposed to paying the levy. To this day some companies still refuse to pay![72]

A further reflection of the decline of Cardiff as a commercial centre in the 1950s came with the news in August 1954 that the Coal & Shipping Exchange (Cardiff) Ltd. had gone into voluntary liquidation; its assets were to be taken over by a new firm, the Cardiff Exchange & Office Co. Ltd. The Association had long rented a room in the Exchange for which an annual rental of £50 was being paid in 1954, but following the inception of the new company, it was decided instead to pay an annual facility fee of £200 to the Chamber of Commerce to cover all administrative, rental and secretarial costs. This new arrangement was approved on 8 October 1954. A new representative committee for all those bodies using the Exchange's facilities was also established at the time, with Raymond Cory being chosen as the Association's representative on this new body.[73]

This new committee was only one of nearly fifty internal and external committees on which members of the Association sat in the mid-1950s. The nationalization of the railways and the docks in 1948 had led to the establishment of numerous different advisory bodies on which the Association was represented, whilst it also sent representatives to no fewer than twelve subsidiary committees of the Chamber of Shipping. All this added up to quite an onerous workload for Association members when one bears in mind that by the mid-1950s they were just over fifty-strong themselves. The amount of general business undertaken by the Association itself, however, had decreased considerably and there were no longer regular monthly meetings of the executive committee, which met about four times a year in the 1950s.[74]

The annual reports of the Association for the early 1950s present contrasting views of the shipping industry from the point of view of Cardiff's shipowners. Whilst general satisfaction was expressed regarding the continuing buoyancy of freight rates, there was general concern about the decline in the coal trade and the ever-decreasing proportion of coal-fired steamers. Coal exports from Cardiff in 1955 amounted to a mere 780,000 tons, whilst it was estimated in the same year that only some 9 per cent of the total world merchant fleet was made up of coal-fired steamers. For the first time ever, concern was also expressed at the growth of competition from tramping fleets operating under flags of convenience such as Liberia or Panama. These concerns were temporarily forgotten in 1956, however, when Egypt's President Nasser decreed the nationalization of the Suez Canal. The canal was closed following the abortive Anglo-French invasion in November and remained closed until

36 Colum T. Tudball, 1957. (By kind permission of Mr Peter C. Tudball, CBE.)

mid-1957. One effect of the crisis was to increase substantially the demand for shipping, and freight rates in the tramp sector soared, recording advances of as much as 40 per cent in some trades. This boom was very short-lived, however; by the end of 1957, freight rates had fallen back substantially, initiating a period of slump that hit tramp shipping with particular severity.[75]

With the benefit of hindsight, it may now be perceived that the Suez crisis of 1956–7 marked a significant juncture in the history of British shipping that in turn had profound implications for shipping at Cardiff. Despite the fact that world trade was increasing, the UK's share in this trade was declining in the face of foreign competition, and by 1959 Britain's merchant fleet had declined to 16.5 per cent of the world total. Another turning-point was reached in 1957 when, for the first time ever, oil outstripped coal as the major provider of energy worldwide. Significant changes in the design of cargo vessels were also manifesting themselves at this time. The traditional shelter-decked, engines-midships tramp of some 7,000–9,000 deadweight tons (whose basic design had remained largely unchanged since about 1910), was being superseded by the engines-aft bulk carrier with a cargo capacity some three times that of the old tramps. The economies of scale that could be achieved with such vessels enabled their owners to compete in the worldwide tramping trades in which they now had to participate if they wished to remain in shipping – but not every owner could afford such vessels.

The slump in freight rates that followed the end of the Suez crisis persisted into the early 1960s, with Cardiff-owned ships once again lying idle on the River Fal. During these years, a number of local shipowners came to the conclusion that the future prospects in the business were far from favourable and decided to withdraw from shipowning. The minutes of Association meetings during the years 1956–64 often make reference to the 'regrettable decision' by some prominent local shipowners to cease trading, amongst them well-known shipping families who had served the Association well, such as Duncan, Gould, Morel and Seager. Attempts were made in the early 1960s to increase the membership of the Association by inviting some of the local dredging firms to join, but to no avail. The decline in membership accelerated sharply after the Suez crisis; whereas there had been sixty-one individual members in 1945, this figure had fallen to thirty by 1965.

Falling membership figures had once more precipitated the Association into financial difficulties by the summer of 1961 and a meeting was called on 11 August to discuss the situation. It was reported that during the previous financial year receipts had amounted to £204, whilst expenditure had totalled £350. The chairman, Leighton Seager, suggested the sale of the remaining sum held in $3\frac{1}{2}$% War Stock; other options raised from the floor included an appeal for financial backing from the Chamber of Commerce.[76] This latter suggestion unconsciously harked back to the foundation of the Association in 1875, when J. H. Wilson had suggested the creation of sectional subcommittees within the Chamber of Commerce to deal with certain aspects of Cardiff's commercial interests. The meeting eventually decided against all of the options discussed and resolved instead to arrange an overdraft whilst a subcommittee was appointed to consider the best solution to the Association's predicament.

The subcommittee made its initial report back to the Association on 6 March 1962, recommending the cessation of the printing of the annual report and the raising of the subscription to eight guineas. There was some doubt expressed as to whether these measures would prove sufficient, and the subcommittee was asked to reconsider its proposals. On 7 June 1962 it reported back once more with a more radical set of proposals, comprising:

1. The sale of a further £450 of $3\frac{1}{2}$% War Stock.
2. Cessation of printing of the annual report.
3. Subscriptions to be maintained at five guineas.
4. A supplementary levy on tonnage owned of a farthing per gross ton up to 30,000 gross tons; an eighth of a penny per gross ton over 30,000 gross tons.
5. Additional voting rights; one vote for each 10,000 gross tons up to 30,000 gross tons; one vote for every 20,000 gross tons over 30,000 gross tons.[77]

These proposals received the unanimous backing of members and it was hoped that the package of measures would secure the Association's financial viability. Whether members realized or not at the time, however, there was great irony in certain aspects of the measures adopted in 1962, as they comprised a levy on tonnage owned and proportional voting rights. Almost exactly fifty years previously, the Association had been split by dissension on these very points, leading to the establishment in 1912 of the rival British Channel Shipowners' Association which was totally opposed to any kind of 'tonnage-weighted' franchise. The latter organization was eventually successful in forcing the adoption of the principle of 'one man, one vote' upon the Cardiff Incorporated Shipowners' Association, leading to reunification in the spring of 1914. In adopting the measures outlined above in 1962, the Association was reverting to a system of franchise very similar to that which had existed prior to 1914, and which had caused so much bitter strife at the time. (It should be noted that, at this time, Sir William Reardon Smith & Sons had a great preponderance of tonnage over all other owners in the Association, and whilst they wished to take an active role in the administration of the Association, they did not want to use this voting power to the exclusion of the wishes of other members. It was also felt to be unfair that they should contribute to the tonnage levy on a uniform gross tonnage basis for their entire fleet.) Nevertheless, it cannot be disputed that the measures adopted under the chairmanship of Desmond Williams in 1962 were urgently necessary and vital to the restoration of the Association's financial viability at the time.

When not preoccupied with resolving internal problems, the Association continued to concern itself with other affairs that affected members in the 1950s and 1960s. Declining trade in the south Wales ports led to proposals to raise dock dues and rationalize dock facilities. Any increases in dock dues were strongly opposed by the Association, who described increases proposed in the summer of 1957 as 'a blank cheque to impose rates under a monopoly which could be most harmful to trading interests . . . the principle should be opposed on a national basis'.[78]

In February 1958, it was announced that there was to be a public inquiry into the proposed increases in March that year, to which the Association was invited to send representatives; in the event, members were content that the representatives of the Chamber of Shipping attending the inquiry should represent the Association's interests.

Later in 1958, proposals were made to close the coal tips on the River Ely at Cardiff and the South Dock at Swansea, proposals that were opposed by the Association's coaster-owning members. During the following year, the closure of both the West Bute and East Bute docks at Cardiff was first mooted, as was a proposal to concentrate what remained of coal exports from south Wales at either Barry or Cardiff. Such proposals were opposed by the Association, not so much from the point of view of coal-exporting facilities, rather the reduction in coal-bunkering facilities that would ensue. There was a general feeling that the south Wales ports were being run down, and the Association demanded 'a new, imaginative and positive approach' from the port authorities.[79] In the event, however, widespread closures followed; the River Ely tips closed in 1962, Penarth Dock in 1963 and the Bute West Dock in 1964.

The latter year also witnessed an event that the founders of the Association would not have believed possible. Despite fierce opposition from the Association, backed by the Chamber of Commerce and the south Wales branch of the Institute of Chartered Shipbrokers, the British Transport Docks Board decided to concentrate coal exports from south Wales at Barry and Swansea. Accordingly, at 6.30 on the morning of 25 August 1964, the little coaster *Farringay* sailed from Cardiff with the last

37   The first Cardiff-owned bulk carrier was Graig Shipping's *Graigwerdd*, completed by Scotts of Greenock in 1964.

official cargo of steam coal to be exported from the port. Cardiff's *raison d'être* as a port slipped away down the Bristol Channel with that final cargo of 'black diamonds'.[80] But if the departure of the *Farringay* marked the end of an era, the years 1963–4 also marked the beginning of another, with the acquisition of bulk carriers by three member companies of the Association; Newport-based Gibbs & Co. took delivery of the 28,600 deadweight ton *Welsh Herald* for their Welsh Ore Carriers subsidiary in April 1963, to be followed by Graig Shipping's 28,370 deadweight ton *Graigwerdd* in August 1964 and Reardon Smith's 30,000 deadweight ton *Australian City* in November that year. These were to be the first of many such vessels to be operated by these firms in subsequent years, marking their commitment at the time to continuing participation in the worldwide tramping trades which experienced a fortunate improvement in freight rates from 1964 onwards.

Ships sailing in the Bristol Channel required pilots to ensure their safe navigation. Proposals to reorganize and amalgamate the various pilotage authorities in the area had been mooted before the Second World War; during the post-war years, they took on something of the nature of a never-ending saga, as efforts at reorganization were quietly, but firmly, rebuffed by the pilots on a number of occasions. It was noted at a meeting held in November 1954 that the question of proposed amalgamation remained unresolved, whilst two years later it was reported to the Association that the pilots had intimated that whilst they were not averse to preliminary discussions, they were not willing to initiate such discussions themselves. In 1959 the Letch Report and Recommendations on the Earnings of Pilots was published; whilst primarily concerned with pilots' salaries, it also noted the desirability of amalgamation and rationalization of pilotage authorities, not least as a means of increasing individual pilots' earnings. The pilots, however, remained cool in their response to such proposals, with Newport pilots turning down a scheme for inter-authority co-operation in the operation of pilot cutters in May 1959.[81]

In June 1962, the Rochdale Committee of Inquiry into the Major Ports of the United Kingdom was published. One of the inquiry's conclusions was that there was an over-capacity of port facilities in south Wales, recommending the closure of Barry Docks as a possible solution. The Association decided not to oppose the notion provided that (as the Rochdale Report suggested) improved dockside equipment and facilities were installed at nearby south Wales ports to compensate for the loss of those at Barry. One wonders what Thomas Roe Thompson would have thought, recalling his eloquent submissions on behalf of the Association to promote the construction of the dock at Barry in the early 1880s! Of more immediate relevance, however, were Rochdale's recommendations on pilotage, which yet again urged amalgamation and proposed the following authorities in the Bristol Channel:

1. Newport and Bristol
2. Port Talbot (ore carriers)
3. Cardiff, Barry and Swansea

These proposals were endorsed by members of the Association, but over two years later the Association was still urging the Ministry of Transport to intervene and demand that the pilots initiate meaningful negotiations on amalgamation. Then in the autumn of 1965, the Ministry of Transport announced its intention to hold an inquiry into pilotage services in the eastern half of the Bristol Channel, to be held on 10–12 November and to be chaired by Rawlings Smith, assistant secretary to Trinity House. The Association sent three representatives to the inquiry, its three delegates to the Newport, Cardiff and Barry pilotage authorities. It came as no great surprise that in his report published in January 1966, Rawlings Smith too recommended amalgamation, but the pilots still demurred. By April 1967 they had at least started preliminary discussions on what the salary scales might be under a unitary authority, but two years later there was still no substantial progress and the Association was particularly critical of the Newport pilots, whom it was alleged had 'reverted to their former antagonism towards full amalgamation'.[82]

Ships arriving at ports in south Wales often also needed tugs, and in a meeting held on 2 November 1961, it was announced to the Association that tug-owners R. & H. J. Rea of London were bringing four tugs into the Bristol Channel to augment the service provided by the local tug-owners. Rea's denied that they were entering into competition, even promising not to undercut local towage rates; but they had been led to believe that there were insufficient tugs available at any one time in the area. Association members welcomed the increased choice of available tugs that this development would afford; within three days, however, they had been invited to a meeting with the Cardiff Steam Tug Owners' Association at which their secretary, G. A. Guy, deplored the development, citing the fact that Rea's had withdrawn from the Bristol Channel in 1938 when trade was unfavourable. Misgivings were also voiced about the need for more tugs in the area at a time of declining shipping activity in south Wales ports. Again, Association members, whilst expressing sympathy with Mr Guy in his predicament, stated that a greater choice of tugs could only be beneficial to shipowners. History was to prove Guy's fears well founded, however, for his company went into voluntary liquidation on 30 June 1963, with his vessels and his firm's goodwill all passing to Rea's.[83]

In March 1966, the proposed establishment of a South Wales Docks Board was announced. Its purpose was to act as a consultative body on which the interests of industry and commerce in south Wales could be represented, and the Association was asked to nominate one member from its ranks to represent the local shipowners. There was some doubt amongst members as to whether or not there was any purpose in establishing a local board because the Association was already represented on the national British Transport Docks Board. It was eventually decided to support the establishment of the new body, which was soon to be put to use by the Association as a result of the strike by the National Union of Seamen which lasted from 16 May until 1 July that summer. Whilst no mention was made of the strike during its duration in Association meetings, it was reported in a meeting held on 14 November 1966 that an application had been made to waive (or at least to reduce) the dock dues levied upon vessels compelled to remain in port as a result of the strike. This application had been rejected by the chief docks manager for south Wales, who argued that the docks themselves had also lost heavily as a result of the strike. It is most indicative of the way in which the trading patterns of Cardiff-owned ships had changed that the Association decided not to pursue the matter, as 'it was not thought that many owners incurred heavy dock rental locally any longer'.[84]

By the beginning of the 1970s, there were just twenty-four individual members belonging to the Association, representing nine shipping

38 Strike-bound vessels in Cardiff Docks, June 1966.

companies that owned 306,650 gross tons of shipping. They met only some three or four times per annum in a few ordinary meetings and in the annual general meeting, which over the years had moved from a date in early January to mid-June. This was a reflection of the fact that there were fewer and fewer matters of local significance to discuss.

It should not be implied from this, however, that all local shipping interests were in a near-moribund state at that time. A number of the constituent companies were in expansive mood, with the Reardon Smith Line, for instance, working in close co-operation with Upper Clyde Shipbuilders to produce the highly successful 26,000 deadweight ton 'Cardiff' class of bulk carriers. Several of these reliable and economic vessels were built for Reardon Smith, with the remaining twenty-four vessels in the class going to numerous other owners worldwide.[85] Indeed, the acquisition of numerous bulk carriers by firms like Reardon Smith and Graig Shipping led to a post-war peak in Cardiff-owned tonnage in the mid-1970s, with almost 350,000 gross tons of shipping under local ownership in 1975, the Association's centenary year.[86] Having enjoyed a period of relatively buoyant freight rates since about 1964, however, the oil price crisis of 1973 triggered off a sharp decline in rates from 1974

39   A 'Cardiff-class' bulk carrier: Reardon Smith's *Tacoma City*, built by Upper Clyde Shipbuilders in 1972, at Cardiff in October 1984. This was to be the last occasion on which a Reardon Smith vessel visited Cardiff.

onwards, which was destined to have a serious effect on Cardiff's remaining shipping interests in ensuing years.

One long-running matter which had occupied the Association over many years was eventually concluded on 1 August 1974 when the South East Wales Pilotage Authority came into existence. Declining trade in the Bristol Channel and the need to acquire new pilot cutters meant that economies became inevitable, accelerating the eventual amalgamation of the Barry, Cardiff and Newport pilots into the new unitary authority.[87] Further changes affecting the Association were noted in a meeting held in February 1975, when the creation of the General Council of British Shipping – an amalgamation of the functions of the Chamber of Shipping and the Shipping Federation – was reported to members. The Association was entitled to send one representative to the GCBS South Western District meetings. Some differences over the sum paid for secretarial services to the Cardiff Chamber of Commerce and Industry, as well as the proportion of the Shipping Levy paid to the same body eventually led to the transfer of the Association's secretarial services to

40 *Nelson received by Admiral Sir John Jervis after the Battle of Cape St Vincent, 14 February, 1797* by Arthur David McCormick. This painting was commissioned by W. J. Tatem in 1916 and was bequeathed to the Association following his tragic death in an air raid upon Weston-super-Mare on 24 June 1942. It now hangs in the Welsh Industrial and Maritime Museum's gallery at 126 Bute Street.

W. R. Henke, local secretary of the GCBS, with effect from 1 January 1978, though the Association maintained its representative on the Chamber of Commerce.[88] Henceforward the Shipping Levy would be divided between the shipowners and the shipbrokers on the basis of a 30:70 division.

It was in May 1983 that the Association first made formal contact with the Welsh Industrial and Maritime Museum. In 1916, W. J. Tatem (later Lord Glanely) had commissioned an oil painting from the Irish painter, Arthur David McCormick, portraying the reception of Horatio Nelson by Admiral Sir John Jervis after the Battle of Cape St Vincent on 14 February 1797. Following Lord Glanely's tragic death in a bombing raid on Weston-super-Mare on 24 June 1942, the painting was bequeathed to the Association. By 1983, Association members felt that the painting should have a new home at the Welsh Industrial and Maritime Museum, and in a reception held at the museum on 11 November 1983, the painting was presented to the curator, Dr. J. Geraint Jenkins, by the Association's chairman, Philip D. Thomas. The museum also mounted a small exhibition entitled 'Cardiff Shipowners' to coincide with the event.

The freight market revived briefly in 1979–80, only to descend to profound troughs again in 1982–3 and 1984–5; this was reflected in the dwindling number of Association members in the 1980s. Both periods of slump saw the obliteration of names famous in Cardiff shipping circles. In August 1983, Evan Thomas, Radcliffe & Co. disposed of the last two vessels of a noted fleet that had been Cardiff's greatest in 1913. Then, on 31 May 1985, came the announcement that the Reardon Smith Line, for so long synonymous with shipowning at Cardiff, was going into voluntary liquidation. The impending demise of the company also raised questions as to the continued viability of a shipowners' association at Cardiff. Of the five remaining companies represented on the Association, two – the Abbey Line Ltd. and John Cory & Sons – possessed no ships; Gibbs & Co. had two small coasters, whilst Geest Line did not play a particularly active role in the Association's affairs. Only Graig Shipping remained with a substantial fleet.

41   **Desmond I. Williams, 1962; 1985–8.**

Desmond I. Williams had succeeded to the chair for the second time at the AGM held on 24 May 1985; with the aim of maintaining the Association's viability in mind, he approached Douglas C. Reid, managing director of Charles M. Willie & Co (Shipping) Ltd., Cardiff, with an invitation to the firm to re-join the Association. Willie's membership had lapsed during the years 1966–77 when the

42   **Douglas C. Reid, 1988–91.**

company had withdrawn from direct shipowning, but in 1978 they had purchased two short-sea traders which became their *Celtic Venture* and *Celtic Endeavour*.[89] The invitation was accepted gratefully and on 23 September 1985, Douglas Reid was elected vice-chairman of the

Association, whilst his co-director Hubert Wilson was elected a member. This placed the Association on a firmer footing on its 110th birthday, but further problems arose in the ensuing year with the impending closure of the local GCBS office in Cardiff, thus depriving the Association of its secretarial services. Faced with this problem, Desmond Williams turned to the curator of the Welsh Industrial and Maritime Museum, Dr Geraint Jenkins, with the suggestion that the museum might take over the Association's secretarial services. The proposal found favour with the museum authorities and the Association's registered office was moved to the museum in July 1986.[90]

As has been noted, the question of 'flagging-out' of ships was discussed by the Association as far back as 1894, but it was to be almost a century before the profound economic pressures affecting the shipping world in the 1980s led Cardiff's remaining owners reluctantly to follow this course of action. Graig Shipping's vessels were transferred to Bermudian registry in 1985–6, whilst Charles M. Willie & Co. adopted Bahamian registry for all but one of their vessels (the *Celtic Challenger*) in 1989–90. Those same economic pressures led other member companies either to withdraw from shipowning, or to decide that there was no viable prospect of re-entering the business; both John Cory & Sons and Gibbs & Co. Ltd. announced their intention of withdrawing from membership of the Association. Moreover, Geest Line ceased membership of the Association following their decision to relocate the UK terminal of their service to the Windward Islands from Barry to Southampton early in 1993.[91]

Still faced with the problem of declining membership, invitations were issued to a number of shipping companies having interests with the Bristol Channel to join the Association in the early 1990s. Of those invited, only one, Curnow Shipping Ltd., of Porthleven, Cornwall, joined in June 1992. The company operates the passenger/cargo liner RMS *St Helena* on the service to St Helena and Cape Town, and has used Cardiff as its UK port of call since 1990. This is the first time that the Association has had a member company operating a deep-sea passenger vessel; the *St Helena* can carry a maximum of 128 passengers. Her imposing yellow funnel bearing Curnow's 'seahorse' motif readily betrays her presence during the visits to her berth at Cardiff's Queen Alexandra Dock.[92]

The number of committees on which the Association has representatives has been reduced dramatically. The restructuring of the GCBS already referred to meant that the south-western district committee of the Council (on which the Association had a representative) ceased to exist. The Association has retained its membership of the GCBS, however, which reverted to using the title 'Chamber of Shipping' from 1993 onwards. The privatization of Associated British Ports in 1982 swept

43   Never to be seen again? Will the *Celtic Challenger*, sold in June 1995, go down in history as the last Cardiff-registered ocean-going merchant vessel?

away many committees, whilst the final chapter in the long-running saga of the pilotage authorities came to an end on 10 October 1988 with the winding-up of the South East Wales Pilotage Authority. Today, the Association is represented only on the Cardiff Chamber of Commerce and Industry Council, out of which body it first grew in 1875.

44   The RMS *St Helena* at Cape Town. She is the first large passenger vessel controlled by a member company in the Association's history. (By kind permission of Curnow Shipping Ltd.)

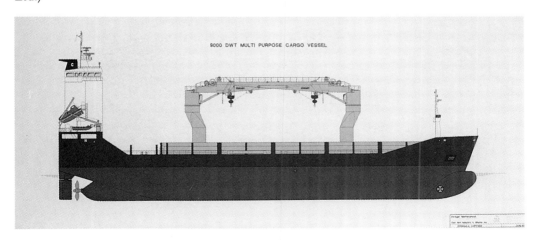

45   A naval architect's elevation of the 'Confidence' class of 9,000 deadweight ton multi-purpose cargo vessels currently being built at a Shanghai shipyard for the consortium comprising Graig Shipping plc and Clipper Shipping of Copenhagen. With a heavy lift capacity of 300 tonnes, these vessels are designed to carry 650 containers at a speed of 16.5 knots. (By kind permission of Graig Shipping plc, Clipper Shipping Group and Carl Bro Industry & Marine.)

46   **In the 1990s, Cardiff-owned ships can still be found plying waters sailed by hundreds of their predecessors. Passing through the Bosporus on her maiden voyage in September 1994 was the *Celtic Ambassador*, built for Charles M. Willie & Co. (Shipping) Ltd. She was the fourth in the first series of multi-purpose vessels built for the firm, since followed by four further 'second-generation' vessels with a capacity for 477 containers and a speed of 15.5 knots. (By kind permission of Charles M. Willie & Co. (Shipping) Ltd.)**

Despite the decline that has occurred, it is most pleasing to be able to note that the two remaining Cardiff-based shipping companies that still belong to the Association are both in dynamic mood, wholeheartedly committed to remaining in shipping. Graig Shipping plc has recently moved away from the dry bulk trades with which it had long been associated, having entered into an agreement with Clipper Shipping of Copenhagen to build an initial series of four 9,000 deadweight ton multi-purpose cargo vessels at a Shanghai shipyard. An option to build a further four vessels has been exercised subsequently by Graig Shipping, bringing the total of newbuildings to eight and they have a further option to extend the series to ten in the not-too-distant future.[93] Charles M. Willie & Co. (Shipping) Ltd. currently operate a fleet of twelve vessels, some of which maintain their regular cargo liner services to Spain and Portugal. They are also presently taking delivery of a second series of four 6,000 deadweight ton multi-purpose vessels from a shipyard at Eregli on the Turkish Black Sea coast, intended for time-charter to Gracechurch Line for their UK–Mediterranean container line service. In fact, with these two companies, Cardiff has the largest newbuilding programme of any port in the UK at the time of writing. As the next millennium approaches, therefore, it is still far too soon to write of the demise of Cardiff as a centre for shipowning.

3 Some Reflections

When the Cardiff Shipowners' Association was incorporated in 1884, its primary aim was defined as being, 'to watch over and defend the interests of shipping'. Perhaps it should more accurately have read 'the interests of shipowners', for the Association was formed by a group of men who not only owned ships, but who believed above all in the values of a competitive economic structure in which the market ruled: it was the market that settled the 'correct' rates for those 'commodities' such as freight rates or bunker prices that influenced their day-to-day existence as shipowners. As such, the Association was consistently implacable in its opposition to additional financial obligations imposed upon shipowners which were perceived to be 'artificial' in origin and which might affect the viability of members' ventures: these included tax increases, increases in dock, light and pilotage dues and increased costs brought about by new legislation. This doctrine of *laissez-faire* prevailed even throughout the difficult inter-war years, when the market's inexorable machinations ruined dozens of Cardiff's less competent shipowners. It should also be recalled that some of those who survived the difficulties of that era poured scorn upon legislations such as the 'Scrap and Build' Acts of the 1930s, perceiving them as attempts to 'buck the markets'.

There were other spheres of activity, however, in which the Association and its members adopted a far more pragmatic attitude, particularly with regard to labour relations. It might have been expected that the Association would have adopted a dogmatic authoritarian line in its attitude towards trades unions and disputes between capital and labour, but this was often not the case. A generally conciliatory attitude was adopted towards the coal trimmers' union, though the Association did attempt to employ non-union trimmers having been out-manoeuvred by the CCTU in 1907. The Seamen's Strike of 1911 (when one might have expected implacable opposition to the forces of organized sea-going labour) saw many Association members expressing guarded support for the notion of trades unionism amongst seamen and a willingness to accede to the NSFU's demands despite the far more dogmatic approach being promoted by the Shipping Federation in London. The Association's more conciliatory approach was prompted admittedly by two main factors: a strong desire to minimize strife on the streets of Cardiff and the commercial imperative to have ships trading at sea at a time of improving freight rates. The social and economic realities of the situation at Cardiff triumphed over more polarized views being projected from beyond the city.

There were other occasions when the Association acted as almost anything but an association. It proved itself unable to put forward a consensus view on the matter of a new dock at Barry in the 1880s, with members presenting conflicting evidence to parliamentary committees of enquiry. The 'schism' of 1912–14 over the Association's system of franchise was badly handled, in that it was allowed to 'snowball' out of all proportion to the root of the problem. It led to the establishment of a nonsensical splinter organization whose long-term effectiveness and viability was highly questionable. The Association also turned something of a blind eye to the highly dubious shipping losses of the years 1905–10, which had such an adverse effect on the probity of Cardiff shipowners on the London insurance market. Decisive action to censure owners involved in these questionable losses could have restored faith in Cardiff shipping and prevented the haemorrhage from local registration that saw many Cardiff-owned ships registered elsewhere on the eve of the First World War.

By today, however, all Cardiff-owned ships are registered elsewhere and the Association that still represents the owners of these vessels is but a shadow of its former self; an annual general meeting now suffices for the conduct of its business. Nevertheless, the Association continues to act on behalf of those owners, communicating with the Chamber of Shipping and the shipping minister requesting elucidation on certain aspects of shipping policy and legislation. It also continues to play a part in the administration of the Cardiff and Newport Shipping Levy Fund. This history should not therefore be regarded as the obituary of the Cardiff and Bristol Channel Incorporated Shipowners' Association, but rather an interpretative account of what has happened hitherto. The Association will exist as long as there are shipowners at the port of Cardiff.

Appendices

APPENDIX 1

The Association's Chairmen

1875–81	Edward S. Hill	Charles Hill & Sons (Bristol)
1882	Edward H. Capper	Capper, Alexander & Co.
1883	John Moore	J. Moore & Co.
1884	Charles E. Stallybrass	C. E. Stallybrass
1885	A. Bernard Tellefsen	Tellefsen & Wills
1886	J. Robert Christie	C. O. Young & Christie
1887	John Guthrie	Barnes, Guthrie & Co.
1888	George H. Wills	Tellefsen & Wills
1889	Thomas Morel	Morel Brothers
1890	Henry Radcliffe	Evan Thomas, Radcliffe & Co.
1891	Sir John Gunn	J. & M. Gunn & Co.
1892	Count Antonio de Lucovich	Lucovich & Co.
1893	John Cory	John Cory & Sons
1894	John H. Wilson	J. H. Wilson & Co.
1895	Philip Turnbull	Turnbull Brothers
1896	William R. Corfield	W. R. Corfield & Co.
1897	W. Watkin Jones	Evan Jones & Co.
1898	Henry Jones	W. & C. T. Jones
1899	Arthur Mawson	Stephens, Mawson & Co.
1900	William Jones	W. & C. T. Jones
1901	Humphrey Wallis	Osborn & Wallis
1902	Edmund Handcock	E. Handcock & Co.
1903	William Anning	Anning Brothers
1904	Daniel Radcliffe	Evan Thomas, Radcliffe & Co.
1905	Hilary B. Marquand	Care & Marquand
1906	George H. Wills	G. H. Wills & Co.
1907	William J. Tatem	W. J. Tatem & Co.
1908	Trevor S. Jones	Jones, Hallett & Co.
1909	John T. Duncan	J. T. Duncan & Co.
1910	Thomas E. Morel	Morel Brothers
1911	William H. Jones	W. & C. T. Jones
1912	A. R. Chenhalls	R. E. Morel & Co.
1913	John Cory	John Cory & Sons
1914	Edward Nicholl	E. Nicholl & Co.
1915	Ralph E. Morel	R. E. Morel & Co.

1916	Robert O. Sanderson	J. & R. O. Sanderson & Co.
1917	William E. Jones	W. & C. T. Jones
1918	Sir William Seager	W. H. Seager & Co.
1919	Lewis Lougher	Lougher & Co.
1920	Thomas H. Mordey	Williams & Mordey
1921	Thomas B. Humphries	Humphries (Cardiff) Ltd.
1922	Frederick Jones	Frederick Jones & Co.
1923	William E. Hinde	W. E. Hinde & Co.
1924	Walter A. Gould	Goulds Steamships & Industrials Ltd.
1925	Daniel Radcliffe	Evan Thomas, Radcliffe & Co.
1926	John W. Duncan	J. T. Duncan & Co.
1927	G. Leighton Seager	W. H. Seager & Co.
1928	Frederick C. Perman	Chellew Steam Navigation Co. Ltd.
1929	Arthur J. Popham	Sir William Reardon Smith & Sons Ltd.
1930	Richard H. Read	Hain Steamship Co. Ltd.
1931	John E. Emlyn-Jones	Emlyn-Jones & Co. Ltd.
1932	John Davies-Kinsey	Howard, Jones Ltd.
1933	Abram R. Watson	Shamrock Shipping Co. Ltd.
1934	J. Elliot Seager, MC	W. H. Seager & Co.
1935	Henry C. Bolter	Evan Thomas, Radcliffe & Co.
1936	John C. Radcliffe	Constants (South Wales) Ltd.
1937	William Gibbs	Gibbs & Co.
1938	Idwal Williams	Idwal Williams & Co.
1939	William Leon	Hall Brothers (Newcastle upon Tyne)
1940	John J. Thomas (to June)	J. J. Thomas & Co.
1940–43	Sir 'Willie' Reardon Smith	Sir William Reardon Smith & Sons Ltd.
1944	Walter T. Gould	W. T. Gould & Co.
1945	Richard P. Care	Care Lines
1946	Sidney P. Richard	Claymore Shipping Co. Ltd.
1947	Richard G. M. Street	South American Saint Line Ltd.
1948	John W. Duncan	J. T. Duncan & Co.
1949	Alexander C. Grant	E. R. Management Ltd.
1950	David I. Rees	Evan Thomas, Radcliffe & Co.
1951	Frederick W. Jones	Frederick Jones & Co.
1952	Brynmor I. Llewellyn	Golden Cross Line Ltd.
1953	Alfred J. Jenkins, MC	John Cory & Sons
1954	Alan J. Reardon Smith	Sir William Reardon Smith & Sons Ltd.
1955	Frederick T. Davey	Claymore Shipping Co. Ltd.
1956	L. Howard Emery	Evan Thomas, Radcliffe & Co.
1957	Colum T. Tudball	Idwal Williams & Co. Ltd.
1958	Raymond Cory	John Cory & Sons
1959	Nigel L. Gibbs	Gibbs & Co. Ltd. (Newport)
1960	Frederick C. Moon	South American Saint Line Ltd.

1961	J. Leighton Seager	W. H. Seager & Co.
1962	Desmond I. Williams	Idwal Williams & Co. Ltd.
1963	P. Treverton Jones	Richard W. Jones & Co. (Newport)
1964–6	A. G. Davies	E. R. Management Ltd.
1966–7	Vivian L. Gibbs	Gibbs & Co. Ltd. (Newport)
1967–8	R. G. Radcliffe	Constants (South Wales) Ltd.
1968–70	R. Haydn Lewis	Evan Thomas, Radcliffe & Co.
1970–2	John P. Reardon Smith	Sir William Reardon Smith & Sons Ltd.
1972–4	John F. Radcliffe	Dovey Shipping Co. Ltd.
1974–6	A. F. Westall	Sir William Reardon Smith & Sons Ltd.
1976–8	T. B. Hamilton	Idwal Williams & Co. Ltd.
1978–80	P. N. L. Gibbs	Gibbs & Co. Ltd. (Newport).
1980–2	Richard W. A. Reardon Smith	Sir William Reardon Smith & Sons Ltd.
1982–4	Phillip D. Thomas	Idwal Williams & Co. Ltd.
1984–5	A. F. Westall	Sir William Reardon Smith & Sons Ltd.
1985–8	Desmond I.Williams	Idwal Williams & Co. Ltd.
1988–91	Douglas C. Reid	Charles M. Willie & Co. (Shipping) Ltd.
1991–4	Richard I. Williams	Idwal Williams & Co. Ltd.
1994–7	Andrew R. Reid	Charles M. Willie & Co. (Shipping) Ltd.
1997–	David Ellis	Graig Shipping plc

(Vice-Chairman: Andrew Bell, Curnow Shipping Ltd.)

APPENDIX 2

The Association's Secretaries

1875–93	Willoughby L. Hawkins	
1893–1931	Willoughby R. Hawkins	Cardiff Chamber
1931–70	Vernon W. Hawkins	of
1970–4	J. C. F. Winckley	Commerce and Industry
1975–7	G. A. S. Turnbull	
1978–80	William R. Henke	
1980–4	R. McKean	General Council of
1984–6	Roy Le Gros	British Shipping
1986–89	J. Geraint Jenkins	Welsh Industrial and
1989–	David Jenkins	Maritime Museum

APPENDIX 3

Companies represented on the Cardiff and Bristol Channel Incorporated Shipowners' Association, 1895–1995

(*Note:* The Association operated a system of individual membership, but the titles of managing ownership firms and partnerships will probably mean more to the modern reader than the names of the principals of those companies. No full list of the original membership for 1875 has survived, whilst changes in company names are noted in successive lists. The headquarters of Association members not based at Cardiff are noted in brackets. The figures for individual membership of the Association are to be found in Appendix 4.)

Companies represented, 1895

M. Angel & Co.
Anning Brothers
Chitham & Henry
M. Cope & Co.
W. R. Corfield & Co.
Cory Brothers
J. Cory & Sons
J. T. Duncan & Co.
Fisher, Renwick & Co. (Newcastle upon Tyne)
Gibbs & Lee
H. B. Gourlay (Newcastle upon Tyne)
J. & M. Gunn & Co.
Guthrie, Heywood & Co.
G. Hallett
E. Handcock & Co.
Hansen, Moore & Moore
C. Hill & Sons (Bristol)
Hoggarth & Woodruff
A. Holland & Co. (London)
J. Holman & Sons (London)
A. J. Hutchins
E. Jones & Co.
W. H. & C. T. Jones
Count de Lucovich
Martin & Marquand
J. Marychurch & Co.
J. Mathias & Son (Aberystwyth)

W. Millburn & Co. (London)
Morel Bros
Osborn & Wallis
Orders & Handford (Newport)
D. & C. Radcliffe
P. Rowe & Sons
C. E. Stallybrass
Stephens, Mawson & Goss
E. Thomas, Radcliffe & Co.
T. R. Thompson
W. J. Tillett & Co.
Turnbull Brothers
Watts, Watts & Co. (London)
G. H. Wills & Co.
J. H. Wilson & Co.
C. O. Young & Christie

Companies represented by the breakaway Bristol Channel Shipowners' Association, 1912–14

Anning Brothers
W. R. Corfield & Co.
Elvidge & Morgan
R. B. Hardy & Co. (West Hartlepool)
E. Jones & Co.
J. W. Pyman & Co.
W. Reardon Smith & Son
P. Rowe & Sons

P. Samuel & Co.
Thomas & Appleton
W. J. Thomas & Co.
W. J. Tillett & Co.
Turnbull Brothers
Williams & Mordey
O. & W. Williams & Co.
G. H. Wills & Co.

Companies represented, 1915

Anning Brothers
W. Badcock & Co.
D. P. Barnett & Co.
T. H. Beynon & Co. Ltd.
Cory Brothers
J. Cory & Sons
C. Cravos & Co.
J. T. Duncan & Co.
Furness, Withy & Co. (London)
J. C. Gould & Co.
Griffiths, Lewis & Co.
A. H. & E. Gunn; previously J. & M.
  Gunn & Co.
E. Hain & Son (St. Ives)
Hall Bros. (Newcastle upon Tyne)
G. Hallett & Co.
E. Handcock & Co.
Harrison Bros. Ltd.
Harries Bros. Ltd. (Swansea).
Hansen, Sons & Co.
C. Hill & Sons (Bristol)
W. E. Hinde & Co.
J. R. Hoggarth & Co.
Humphries (Cardiff) Ltd.
T. Jack & Co. (Larne)
Jenkins Brothers
E. Jenkins & Co.
F. Jones & Co.
R. W. Jones & Co. (Newport)
W. & C. T. Jones; previously W. H. &
  C. T. Jones
Kestell Brothers
F. H Lambert, Barnett & Co.
L. Lougher & Co.
Martin & Marquand

Martyn, Martyn & Co. (Newport)
J. Mathias & Sons (Aberystwyth &
  Cardiff)
A. & W. Matthew
Monroe, Rutherford & Co.
W. Monroe & Co.
Morel Ltd.
R. E. Morel & Co.
Morgan & Cadogan Ltd.
Neale & West Ltd.
E. Nicholl & Co.
Orders & Handford (Newport)
Osborn & Wallis
Palin-Evans & Co. Ltd.
J. W. Pyman & Co.
Pyman, Watson & Co.
C. Radcliffe & Co.
W. Reardon Smith & Son
Renwick,Wilton & Co. (Dartmouth)
P. Samuel & Co. Ltd.
J. & R. O. Sanderson (West
  Hartlepool)
W. H. Seager & Co.
Sivewright, Bacon & Co.
  (Manchester)
C. E. Stallybrass
W. T. Symonds & Co.
W. J. Tatem Ltd.
Thomas, Appleton & Co.
Thomas, Stephens & Wilson
E. Thomas, Radcliffe & Co.
J. J. Thomas & Co.
T. R. Thompson
W. J. Tillett & Co.
Turnbull Brothers.
W. Turpin & Co.
Watts, Watts & Co. (London)
Williams & Mordey
O. & W. Williams & Co.
G. H. Wills & Cory Ltd.

Companies represented, 1935

Ambrose, Davies & Matthews
  (Swansea)
Anning Brothers

B. & S. Shipping Co. Ltd.
D. P. Barnett & Co.
R. P. Care & Co. Ltd.
Chellew Navigation Co. Ltd.
    (London)
Chine Shipping Co. Ltd.
C. L. Clay & Co.
M. Constant & Co. (London &
    Cardiff)
Cory Brothers
J. Cory & Sons
C. Cravos & Co.
J. T. Duncan & Co.
Emlyn-Jones, Griffiths & Co; previ-
    ously Jones & Williams
Gibbs & Co.
W. T. Gould & Co.
Gueret, Llewellyn & Merrett
Hain Steamship Co. Ltd.; previously
    E. Hain & Son
Hall Brothers (Newcastle upon Tyne)
T. Jack & Co. (Larne)
F. Jones & Co.
R. W. Jones & Co. (Newport)
L. Lougher & Co. Ltd.
Martyn, Martyn & Co. Ltd.
Morel Ltd.
Neale & West Ltd.
Pyman Brothers (London)
Sir W. Reardon Smith & Sons Ltd.
Sir R. Ropner & Co. Ltd. (West
    Hartlepool)
W. H. Seager & Co. Ltd.
W. J. Tatem Ltd.
E. Thomas, Radcliffe & Co.
J. J. Thomas (Bute Docks) Ltd.; previ-
    ously J. J. Thomas & Co.
Turnbull Brothers
I. Williams & Co.
Wing Line Ltd.

Companies represented, 1955

Ampleforth Steamship Co. Ltd.; pre-
    viously C. Cravos & Co.
Bromage Shipping Co. Ltd.

R. P. Care & Co. Ltd.
Chellew Navigation Co. Ltd.,
    (London)
Claymore Shipping Co. Ltd.; previ-
    ously C. L. Clay & Co.
Constants (South Wales) Ltd.; previ-
    ously M. Constant & Co.
J. Cory & Sons
Wm. Cory & Sons
J. T. Duncan & Co.
F. S. Dawson Ltd.
E. R. Management Co. Ltd.
Sir James German & Son Ltd.
Gibbs & Co. (Newport)
Golden Cross Line Ltd.
W. T. Gould & Co. Ltd.,
Hall Brothers (Newcastle upon Tyne)
J. & C. Harrison Ltd. (London)
F. Jones & Co.
R. W. Jones & Co. (Newport)
Lambert Bros. Ltd.
Laverton Steamship Co. Ltd.
Lovering & Sons Ltd.
F. W. Moorsom & Co.
Neale & West Ltd.
Sir W. Reardon Smith & Sons Ltd.
Rogers & Bright (South Wales) Ltd.
W. H. Seager & Co. Ltd.
Sessions & Sons Ltd.
Shamrock Shipping Co. Ltd. (Larne);
    previously T. Jack & Co.
South American Saint Line Ltd.; pre-
    viously B. & S. Shipping Co. Ltd.
E. Thomas, Radcliffe & Co.
M. Whitwill & Son (Bristol)
I. Williams & Co.

Companies represented, 1975

J. Cory & Sons
Dovey Shipping & Industrial Holdings
    Ltd.; previously Constants (South
    Wales) Ltd.
Geest Line
Gibbs & Co. (Newport)
F. Jones & Co.

Sir W. Reardon Smith & Sons Ltd.
E. Thomas, Radcliffe & Co.
I. Williams & Co. Ltd.
C. M. Willie & Co. (Shipping) Ltd.;
  previously Bromage Shipping Co.
  Ltd.

Companies represented, 1995

The Abbey Line Ltd.; previously
  F. Jones & Co.
Curnow Shipping Ltd. (Porthleven,
  Cornwall)
Graig Shipping plc; previously
  I. Williams & Co. Ltd.
Charles M. Willie & Co. (Shipping)
  Ltd.

APPENDIX 4

Individual membership figures of the Association

Year	Number	Year	Number
1876	N/A	1941	59
1881	N/A	1946	61
1886	N/A	1951	56
1891	78	1956	54
1896	72	1961	42
1901	86	1966	30
1906	89	1971	24
1911	93	1976	20
1916	147	1981	27
1921	148	1986	22
1926	110	1991	13
1931	84	1996	12
1936	52		

APPENDIX 5

Gross tonnages and numbers of Cardiff-owned ships, 1875–1995

(*Note:* this list gives the aggregate gross tonnage and numbers of merchant vessels owned by companies having their registered office at Cardiff, regardless of vessels' port of registry. It does not comprise tugs, dredgers nor vessels managed in wartime.)

Year	*Gross tonnage*	*Number*
1875	57,115	122
1880	138,423	184
1885	250,161	238
1890	251,141	183
1895	309,207	195
1900	401,275	209
1905	565,160	256
1910	716,803	253
1915	863,015	290
1920	807,450	272
1925	913,204	339
1930	887,798	284
1935	519,361	140
1940	565,475	164
1945	233,259	68
1950	299,903	65
1955	308,872	50
1960	269,962	31
1965	235,815	24
1970	306,650	22
1975	343,989	20
1980	223,261	14
1985	190,222	10
1990	114,750	13
1995	25,564	12

Source: Lloyd's Registers.

APPENDIX 6

Committees upon which Association members served in 1905 and 1955

(*Note:* This appendix is included to give readers some idea of the numerous responsibilities shouldered by Association members. The figures in brackets indicate the number of representatives sent by the Association to sit on each committee.)

1905

1. *Internal Committees of the Association*
Executive Committee (9)
Welsh Coal Charter Party Revision Committee (3)
Towage Committee (3)
Pilotage Committee (5)

2. *Other Organizations*
Chamber of Shipping (1)
The Shipping Federation Ltd., London (1)
The Shipping Federation Ltd., Cardiff District (7)
Cardiff Local Marine Board (6)
Cardiff Trimmers' Board (2)
Cardiff Pilotage Authority (3)
Barry Pilotage Authority (6)
Committee of Lloyd's Register of Shipping (1)
Arbitrators on the Welsh Coal Charter Party (2)
Arbitrators on Bunker Trimming Tariffs (2)
Shipowners' Parliamentary Committee (1)

1955

1. *Internal Committees of the Association*
Executive Committee (22)
Coal Charter Revision Committee (3)
Towage Committee (3)
Pilotage Committee (5)
Training Committee (2)
Coal Loading Hours Committee (8)

2. *Chamber of Shipping Committees*
Council (1)
General Council of British Shipping (2)
Deep Sea Tramps Standing Committee (4)
Deep Sea Tramps Co-operative Committee (1)
Baltic and Intermediate Tramp Standing Committee (2)
Coasting and Home Trade Tramp Standing Committee (3)
Documentary Committee (2)
Pilotage Committee (2)
Defence of Merchant Shipping Committee (1)
Joint Ports Committee (1)
Joint Fuel Committee (3)
Lighthouse Advisory Committee (1)

3. *Other Organizations*
The Shipping Federation Ltd., Cardiff District (7)
The National Maritime Board, Cardiff District (3)
South Wales Area Trimming Board (5)
Cardiff Pilotage Authority (3)
Barry Pilotage Authority (6)
Port Talbot Pilotage Authority (3)
Cardiff Local Marine Board (6)

Management Committee of the Cardiff and Port Talbot Riggers' Clearing Houses (7)

Cardiff Joint Control Board for Dock Pilots, Boatmen and Riggers (12)

Employers' Clearing House, Cardiff (10)

Joint Control Board of the Cardiff, Penarth and Barry Coal Trimmers (6)

Committee of Lloyd's Register of Shipping (3)

Mercantile Marine Welfare Committee (1)

Cardiff Technical College Shipping Industry Advisory Committee (3)

Cardiff Technical College Advisory Committee on Commerce (1)

Industrial Association of Wales and Monmouthshire (1)

Cardiff Port Consultative Committee (1)

British Ships Adoption Society (1)

Port of Cardiff Committee on Fire Prevention and Fire Fighting on Ships in Port (1)

Cardiff Port User's Committee (3)

Transport User's Consultative Committee for Wales (2)

Port of Barry Explosives Committee (1)

Port of Cardiff Explosives Committee (1)

Coal Exchange Representatives Committee (1)

APPENDIX 7

Ships built for Cardiff shipowners under the terms of the British Shipping (Assistance) Act, 1935 ('Scrap and Build')

Starcross	4,693 g.t.	1936	Anning Brothers
St Helena	4,313 g.t.	1936	
St Margaret	4,312 g.t.	1936	B. & S. Shipping Co. Ltd.
St Clears	4,312 g.t.	1936	
St Rosario	4,312 g.t.	1937	
Nailsea Moor	4,926 g.t.	1937	
Nailsea Manor	4,926 g.t.	1937	E. R. Management & Co. Ltd.
Nailsea Court	4,946 g.t.	1936	
Nailsea Meadow	4,946 g.t.	1937	
Bradford City (m.v.)	4,952 g.t.	1936	Sir W. Reardon Smith & Sons Ltd.
Cornish City (m.v.)	4,952 g.t.	1936	
	51,840 g.t.		

Ships built for Cardiff shipowners under the terms of the British Shipping (Assistance) Bill, 1939

St Essylt (m.v.)	5,634 g.t.	1941 loan	South American Saint Line Ltd.
Daydawn	4,768 g.t.	1940 loan	Claymore Shipping Co Ltd.
Ottinge	2,870 g.t.	1940 grant	Constants (South Wales) Ltd.
Beignon (m.v.)	5,218 g.t.	1939 grant	Morel Ltd.
Catrine (m.v.)	5,218 g.t.	1940 grant	
Atlantic City (m.v.)	5,188 g.t.	1941 grant	
Eastern City (m.v.)	5,188 g.t.	1941 grant	Sir W. Reardon Smith & Sons Ltd.
Madras City	5,092 g.t.	1940 grant	
Orient City	5,092 g.t.	1940 grant	
Winkleigh	5,468 g.t.	1940 grant	W. J. Tatem Ltd.
Graiglas	4,312 g.t.	1940 grant	Idwal Williams & Co. Ltd.
	54,042 g.t.		

Source: David Burrell, *Scrap and Build* (World Ship Society, Kendal, 1983).

Notes

Chapter 1 Birth, Growth and Dissent, 1875–1918

[1]   Robin Craig, 'The Ports and Shipping, c. 1750–1914' in Glanmor Williams (ed.), *Glamorgan County History, Vol. 5, Industrial Glamorgan* (Cardiff, 1980), p.512.

[2]   *Ibid.*; for gross tonnages, see Appendix 5.

[3]   *Cardiff Times*, 22 May 1875.

[4]   *Cardiff Times*, 19 June 1875.

[5]   *Cardiff Times*, 21 August 1875.

[6]   *Western Mail*, 20 October 1875.

[7]   Chamber of Shipping, Annual Reports, 1879–88.

[8]   Iorwerth W. Prothero, 'The Port and Railways of Barry' in Donald Moore (ed.), *Barry: The Centenary Book* (Barry, 1984), pp.222–5.

[9]   House of Lords Record Office, Minutes of Evidence to House of Commons Select Committees, 11 April 1883.

[10] *Ibid.*, 4 May 1883.

[11] John Morel Gibbs, *Morels of Cardiff: The History of a Family Shipping Firm* (Cardiff, 1982), pp. 169, 170.

[12] House of Lords Records Office, Minutes of Evidence to House of Lords Select Committees, 6 July 1883.

[13] *Ibid.*

[14] Iorwerth W. Prothero, *op.cit.* pp.224, 225.

[15] Glamorgan Archives Service (hereinafter GAS), D/D Com/C 3, Memorandum and Articles of Association, 1884.

[16] *Ibid.*

[17] Craig, *loc.cit.*

[18] GAS, D/D Com/C 3, Annual Reports, 1893, 1894, 1895.

[19] *Ibid.*

[20] Peter J. Stuckey, *The Sailing Pilots of the Bristol Channel* (Newton Abbot, 1977), p.9.

[21] GAS, D/D Com/C 3, Annual Report, 1909.

[22] *Ibid.*

[23] Stuckey, *op.cit.*, pp.136, 137.

[24] GAS, D/D Com/C 3, Annual Report, 1905.

[25] Martin Daunton, 'The Cardiff Coal Trimmers' Union, 1898–1914', *Llafur*, vol.2, no.3, 1978, p.11.

[26] *Ibid.*, pp. 12–14.

[27] Eric J. Hobsbawm, *Labouring Men: Studies in the History of Labour* (London, 1964), p.214.

[28] GAS, D/D Com/C 3, Annual Report, 1897.

[29] *Ibid.*, Minute Book, 1903–10.

[30] *Ibid.*

[31] Daunton, *op.cit.*, p.15.

[32] Neil Evans, 'Cardiff's Labour Traditions', *Llafur*, vol.4, no.2., 1985, p.78.

33   L. H. Powell, *The Shipping Federation: A History of the First Sixty Years, 1890–1950* (London, 1950), p.136.

34   Arthur Marsh and Victoria Ryan, *The Seamen – A History of the National Union of Seamen* (Oxford, 1989), pp.36, 50.

35   GAS, D/D Com/C 3, Annual Report, 1906.

36   *Ibid.*, Minute Books, 1903–10.

37   Neil Evans, ' "A Tidal Wave of Impatience": The Cardiff General Strike of 1911', in G. H. Jenkins and J. B. Smith (eds.), *Politics and Society in Wales, 1840–1922: Essays in Honour of Ieuan Gwynedd Jones* (Cardiff, 1988), p.142.

38   GAS, D/D Com/C 3, Minute Book, 1910–15.

39   Edward Tupper, *Seamen's Torch: The Life Story of Captain Edward Tupper* (London, 1938), p.51.

40   GAS, D/D Com/C 3, Minute Book, 1910–15.

41   Marsh and Ryan, *op.cit.*, pp.55–6.

42   Neil Evans, *op.cit.*, p.147.

43   GAS, D/D Com/C 3, Minute Book, 1910–15.

44   Neil Evans, *op.cit*, pp.149–52.

45   GAS, D/D/ Com/C 3, Minute Book, 1910–15.

46   *Ibid.*

47   Neil Evans, *op.cit.*, pp.157, 158.

48   GAS, D/D Com/C3, Annual Report, 1906, Minute Books, 1903–10.

49   *Report of the Select Committee on the Manning of Merchant Ships, Parliamentary Papers XL–XLI, 1896.*

50   *Ibid.*

51   *Ibid.*

52   *Ibid.*

53   GAS, D/D Com/C 3, Minute Book, 1903–10.

54   Jess Baillie, 'Board of Trade Shipping Inquiries, 1875–1935', in *Annual Report of the Glamorgan Archivist, 1989,* p.30.

55   *Ibid..*

56   Craig, *op.cit.*, p.502.

57   Baillie, *op.cit.*, p.31.

58   GAS, D/D Com/C 3, Minute Book, 1903–10 .

59   *Ibid.*, Annual Report, 1908.

60   David Masters, *Crimes of the High Seas* (London, 1936), p.158.

61   Craig, *op. cit.*, p.502.

62   See Paul M. Heaton, *Reardon Smith Line: The History of a South Wales Shipping Venture* (Risca, 1984), p.24.

63   GAS, D/D Com/C 3, Minute Book, 1903–1910.

64   *Ibid.*, Annual Reports, 1875, 1903.

65   *Ibid.*, Minute Book, 1890–1903.

66   *Ibid.*, Minute Book, 1910–15.

67   *Ibid.*

68   Public Record Office, B.T. 31/13957/123706.

69   GAS, D/D Com/C 3, Minute Book, 1910–1915.

70   *Ibid.*

71   David Burrell, 'Shipping Economics' in Robert Gardiner (ed.), *The Golden Age of Shipping: The Classic Merchant Ship, 1900–1960* (London, 1994) p.167.

72   GAS, D/D Com/C 3, Annual Report, 1915.

73   *Ibid.*, 1916–18.

74   *Ibid.*, 1917.

[75]   Paul M. Heaton, *Tatems of Cardiff* (Risca, 1987), pp.23, 24.
[76]   GAS, D/D Com/C 3, Annual Reports, 1916, 1917.
[77]   T. C. Wignall, *The Life of Commander Sir Edward Nicholl* (London, 1921), p.134.

Chapter 2   The Long Decline: 1918 to the Present Day

[1]   D. Jeffrey Morgan, 'Boom and Slump – Shipowning at Cardiff, 1919–1921', *Cymru a'r Môr/Maritime Wales*, no.12, 1989, pp.126–51. The opening passages of this chapter draw heavily upon this outstanding article, based upon the author's 1987 M.A. thesis.
[2]   GAS, D/D Com/C 3, Annual Report, 1918.
[3]   Morgan, *op. cit.*, pp.129,130.
[4]   GAS, D/D Com/C 3, Annual Report, 1917.
[5]   *Ibid.*, 1919.
[6]   W. H. Mitchell and L. A. Sawyer, *British Standard Ships of World War 1* (Liverpool, 1968), pp.133–5.
[7]   Morgan, *op. cit.*, p.138.
[8]   *Ibid.*, p.130.
[9]   *Syren and Shipping*, 11 February 1920.
[10]   GAS, D/D Com/C 3, Annual Report, 1919.
[11]   *Ibid.*
[12]   Morgan, *op. cit.*
[13]   Public Record Office, B.T.31/16922/75355.
[14]   Public Record Office, B.T.31/22900/140897.
[15]   Anon., *Cardiff: A Commercial and Industrial Centre* (Cardiff, 1919).
[16]   Morgan, *op. cit.*, p.135.
[17]   GAS, D/D Com/C 3, Annual Report, 1920.
[18]   Martin Daunton, *Coal Metropolis: Cardiff, 1870–1914* (Leicester, 1977), p.227.
[19]   Morgan, *op. cit.*, p.139.
[20]   GAS, D/D Com/C 3, Annual Report, 1921.
[21]   Anon., 'Cardiff – Shipping and Shipowning', *Cardiff 1921* (*Syren and Shipping*, London, 1921), pp.51–3.
[22]   J. Geraint Jenkins and David Jenkins, *Cardiff Shipowners* (Cardiff, 1986), pp.64, 70, 71.
[23]   GAS, D/D Com/C 3, Annual Report, 1922.
[24]   *Ibid.*, Minute Book, 1918–24.
[25]   *Ibid.*, Annual Report, 1925.
[26]   *Ibid.*, 1929.
[27]   For a full account of Owen Williams's shipowning career, see David Jenkins, *Owen and Watkin Williams of Cardiff: The Golden Cross Line* (World Ship Society, Kendal, 1991).
[28]   GAS, D/D Com/C 3, Annual Report, 1927.
[29]   *Ibid.*
[30]   *Ibid.*, 1925.
[31]   *Ibid.*, 1926.
[32]   *Ibid.*, Minute Book, 1918–24.
[33]   *Ibid.*, Annual Reports, 1927, 1928.
[34]   See Peter Bennett and David Jenkins, *Welsh Ports of the Great Western Railway* (Cardiff, 1994) pp.7–10.
[35]   GAS, D/D Com/C 3, Minute Book, 1918–24.

36   *Ibid.*, Annual Report, 1929.
37   *Ibid.*, 1930; see also Appendix 5.
38   *Lloyd's Daily Shipping Index*, 22 June 1933.
39   GAS, D/D Com/C3, Annual Report, 1931.
40   David Burrell, *Scrap and Build* (World Ship Society, Kendal, 1983), p.8. The following passages rely heavily on this exemplary study.
41   *Ibid.*, pp.9, 10.
42   GAS, D/D Com/C 3, Minute Book, 1932–42.
43   See Appendix 7.
44   GAS, D/D Com/C 3, Minute Book, 1932–42.
45   *Ibid.*, Annual Report, 1936.
46   *Ibid.*, 1937.
47   *Ibid.*
48   Burrell, *op. cit.*, p.11.
49   *Ibid.*, p.12.
50   *Ibid.*, p.11.
51   See Appendix 7.
52   See Appendix 2.
53   GAS, D/D Com/C 3, Annual Report, 1936.
54   *Ibid.*, 1930, 1932.
55   *Ibid.*, Minute Book, 1924–31.
56   *Ibid.*, 1932–42.
57   *Ibid.*
58   Paul M. Heaton, *Welsh Blockade Runners in the Spanish Civil War* (Risca, 1985), provides a comprehensive account of the role of Welsh-owned ships in the conflict.
59   GAS, D/D Com/C 3, Minute Book, 1932–42.
60   David Burrell, 'Shipping Economics', in Robert Gardiner (ed.), *The Golden Age of Shipping: The Classic Merchant Ship, 1900–1960* (London, 1994), pp.172–3.
61   GAS, D/D Com/C 3, Minute Book, 1932–42.
62   *Ibid.*
63   *Ibid.*, 1942–57.
64   Bernard Edwards, *They Sank the Red Dragon* (Cardiff, 1987), pp. 5–7.
65   GAS, D/D Com/C 3, Minute Book, 1942–57.
66   John de S. Winser, *The 'D-Day' Ships* (World Ship Society, Kendal, 1994), *passim.*
67   GAS, D/D Com/C 3, Annual Reports, 1945–7.
68   *Ibid.*; see also Appendix 5.
69   Burrell, 'Shipping Economics', p.173.
70   J. Geraint Jenkins, *Evan Thomas, Radcliffe: A Cardiff Shipowning Company* (Cardiff, 1982), pp. 71–4.
71   G.A.S, D/D Com/C 3, Minute Book, 1942–57.
72   *Ibid.*
73   *Ibid.*
74   See Appendices 4 and 6.
75   GAS, D/D Com/C 3, Annual Reports, 1950–7.
76   Minute Book, 1956–70.
77   *Ibid.*
78   *Ibid.*
79   *Ibid.*
80   *South Wales Echo*, 25 August 1964.
81   Minute Book, 1956–70.
82   *Ibid.*

83 W. J. Harvey and K. Turrell, *Empire Tugs* (World Ship Society, Kendal, 1988), pp.105, 149.
84 Minute Book, 1956–70.
85 Harry Spong, 'Ships of the "Cardiff" Class', *Ships Monthly*, November 1982, pp.26–9.
86 See Appendix 5.
87 GAS, South East Wales Pilotage Authority papers, 1994/68: personal recollections, Mr Philip D. Thomas.
88 Minute Book, 1975–85.
89 Paul M. Heaton, 'A Celtic Venture', *Sea Breezes*, vol.53, no.403, July 1979, pp.409–22.
90 Minute Book, 1975–86.
91 *Ibid.*
92 Ronnie Eriksen, *St Helena Lifeline* (Coltishall, 1994).
93 *Lloyd's List*, 21 December 1995; information supplied by Mr Desmond I. Williams.

Bibliography

1. Archival and Documentary Sources

Chamber of Shipping, London

Annual Reports.

Glamorgan Archive Service, Cardiff

Annual Reports.
Cardiff & Bristol Channel Incorporated Shipowners' Association records.
Cardiff Chamber of Commerce records.
South-East Wales Pilotage Authority papers.
Statutory Shipping Registers of the Port of Cardiff.

House of Lords Record Office, Westminster

Minutès of Evidence to House of Commons Select Committee on the Barry
    Dock and Railway Bill, April 1883.
Minutes of Evidence to House of Lords Select Committee on the Barry Dock
    and Railway Bill, July 1883.

Public Record Office, Kew, London

Defunct companies files.

2. Newspapers and Journals

Cardiff and South Wales Journal of Commerce
Cardiff Times
Cymru a'r Môr / Maritime Wales
Llafur
Lloyd's Daily Shipping Index
Lloyd's List
Maritime Review
Sea Breezes
Ships Monthly
South Wales Daily News
South Wales Echo
Syren and Shipping
Western Mail

3. Printed Books

British Vessels lost at Sea, 1914–1918 (HMSO, 1919).

British Vessels lost at Sea, 1939–45, (HMSO, 1947).

Lloyd's Registers (various dates).

Mercantile Navy Lists (various dates).

Parliamentary Papers XL–XLI, 1896 (Report of the Select Committee on the Manning of Merchant Ships).

Anon., *Cardiff: A Commercial and Industrial Centre* (Cardiff, 1919).

Anon., *Cardiff, 1921* (*Syren and Shipping*, London, 1921).

Bennett, Peter, and David Jenkins, *Welsh Ports of the Great Western Railway* (Cardiff, 1994).

Burrell, David, *Scrap and Build* (World Ship Society, Kendal, 1983).

Daunton, Martin, *Coal Metropolis: Cardiff, 1870–1914* (Leicester, 1977).

Davies, John, *Cardiff and the Marquesses of Bute* (Cardiff, 1981).

Edwards, Bernard, *They Sank the Red Dragon* (Cardiff, 1987).

Eriksen, Ronnie, *St. Helena Lifeline* (Coltishall, 1994).

Gibbs, John Morel, *Morels of Cardiff: The History of a Family Shipping Firm* (Cardiff, 1982).

Harvey, W. J., and K. Turrell, *Empire Tugs* (World Ship Society, Kendal, 1988).

Heaton, Paul M., *Welsh Blockade Runners in the Spanish Civil War* (Risca, 1985).

Heaton, Paul M., *Reardon Smith Line: The History of a South Wales Shipping Venture* (Risca, 1984).

Heaton, Paul M., *Tatems of Cardiff* (Risca 1987).

Hill, J. C. G., *Shipshape and Bristol Fashion* (Bristol, 1951).

Hobsbawm, Eric J., *Labouring Men: Studies in the History of Labour* (London, 1964).

Jenkins, David, *Owen and Watkin Williams of Cardiff: The Golden Cross Line* (World Ship Society, Kendal, 1991).

Jenkins, J. Geraint, *Evan Thomas, Radcliffe: A Cardiff Shipowning Company* (Cardiff, 1982).

Jenkins, Geraint J., and David Jenkins, *Cardiff Shipowners* (Cardiff, 1986).

Marsh, Arthur, and Victoria Ryan, *The Seamen: A History of the National Union of Seamen* (Oxford, 1989).

Masters, David, *Crimes of the High Seas* (London, 1936).

Mitchell, W. H., and L. A. Sawyer, *British Standard Ships of World War I* (Liverpool, 1968).

Moore, Donald (ed.), *Barry: The Centenary Book* (Barry, 1984).

Powell, L. H., *The Shipping Federation: A History of the First Sixty Years, 1890–1950* (London, 1950).

Stuckey, Peter J., *The Sailing Pilots of the Bristol Channel* (Newton Abbot, 1977).

Tupper, Edward, *Seamen's Torch: The Life Story of Captain Edward Tupper* (London, 1938).

Wignall, T. C., *The Life of Commander Sir Edward Nicholl* (London, 1921).

Williams, Desmond I., *Seventy Years in Shipping* (Cowbridge, 1989).

Williams, John, *Was Wales Industrialised?* (Llandysul, 1995).

Winser, John de S., *The 'D-day' Ships* (World Ship Society, Kendal, 1994).

4. Articles

Baillie, Jess, 'Board of Trade Shipping Inquiries, 1875–1935', in *Annual Report of the Glamorgan Archivist*, 1989.

Burrell, David, 'Shipping Economics', in Robert Gardiner (ed.), *The Golden Age of Shipping: The Classic Merchant Ship, 1900–1960* (London, 1994).

Craig, Robin, 'The Ports and Shipping, *c*.1750–1914', in Glanmor Williams (ed.), *Glamorgan County History*, Vol. 5, *Industrial Glamorgan* (Cardiff, 1980).

Daunton, Martin, 'The Cardiff Coal Trimmers' Union, 1898–1914', *Llafur*, vol.2, no.3, 1978.

Evans, Neil, 'Cardiff's Labour Traditions', *Llafur*, vol.4, no.2, 1985.

Evans, Neil, 'A Tidal Wave of Impatience: the Cardiff General Strike of 1911', in G. H. Jenkins and J. B. Smith (eds.), *Politics and Society in Wales, 1840–1922: Essays in Honour of Ieuan Gwynedd Jones* (Cardiff, 1988.)

Heaton, Paul M., 'A Celtic Venture', *Sea Breezes*, vol.53, no.403, July 1979.

Morgan, D. Jeffrey, 'Boom and Slump – Shipowning at Cardiff, 1919–1921', *Cymru a'r Môr / Maritime Wales*, No.12, 1989.

Prothero, Iorwerth W., 'The Port and Railways of Barry', in Donald Moore (ed.), *Barry: The Centenary Book* (Barry, 1984.).

Spong, Harry, 'Ships of the "Cardiff" class', *Ships Monthly*, November 1982.

Index